HITCHED

HITCHED

The Modern Woman and Arranged Marriage

NANDINI KRISHNAN

RANDOM HOUSE INDIA

Published by Random House India in 2013

1

Copyright © Nandini Krishnan 2013

Random House Publishers India Private Limited
Windsor IT Park, 7th Floor
Tower-B, A-1, Sector-125
Noida 201301, UP

Random House Group Limited
20 Vauxhall Bridge Road
London SW1V 2SA
United Kingdom

978 81 8400 373 4

The names of some of the interviewees have been changed
to protect their privacy.

Typeset in Elegant Garamond BT by R. Ajith Kumar

Printed and bound in India by Replika Press Private Limited

To Maruthi, Babu Mama and Ma

Contents

Contents

Contents

Introduction

The idea for this book first took root over a phone call. Meru Gokhale, to whom I had once spoken of how I want to write a satire on Indian marriages, asked me if I wanted to write a serious book on arranged marriage. She refused to believe both that she hadn't woken me up, and that I wasn't qualified to write it. She asked me to think about it for a day or two, and get back in touch. I was in a dilemma. I'd known I wanted to work with Meru since I had first met her, not only because of the wonderfully fun conversations we've had, but because I've simply loved every book she has edited. I knew she is that rare breed of editor who can tap the right buttons in a writer's head without the latter even realizing it. But I didn't see how I could write a non-fiction work on arranged marriage.

As I thought about the book, I thought mostly of my own brushes with arranged marriage. My mother would rather regularly, in my early twenties, tell me hesitantly that there was 'an offer'. I would usually roll my eyes and say, 'What's the bid?' Profiles would be emailed to me, and grammatically incorrect emails from prospective grooms' parents forwarded.

Most of these contained details of the 'boy's' exam results from high school to college, his salary, his designation and his personality—'outgoing', 'friendly', 'cheerful', 'vivacious', and in one case, inexplicably, 'rambunctious'. It was hard enough to find a 'prospect' whose hairline could be spotted, whose neck wasn't caked with powder and who didn't sport a Chulbul Pandey moustache. It was harder to find someone who didn't think Orhan Pamuk was the name of a book.

Most of my friends and I had spent our twenties whining either about our boyfriends, or about the sort of men we were being put in touch with. A lot of those accounts could go into a work of fiction. But how would I find people who had had arranged marriages, and who were willing to talk about them? And then, I realized that many of my friends—intelligent, smart, funny women—had eventually taken the 'arranged' route, and several of them were so happy that I'd even forgotten they found their husbands through a maze of matrimonial ads, horoscopes and awkward conversations.

There are, of course, those who are firmly opposed to the idea of arranged marriage. One of my friends calls it 'mercenary', and says she knows people who marry based solely on the career progress and bank balance of their prospective spouses. There are those who are so resentful of the process, and the demand for 'tall, slim, fair, beautiful, intelligent working' women who must also cook well, that they respond with physical specifications of their own. There are those who are disillusioned and frustrated by the process. There are those whose marriages were technically arranged, but read like love stories.

I began to put down a structure for the book, and realized it wasn't going to be either didactic or dry. Marriage is one of the most crucial aspects of a woman's life—whether she chooses to have an arranged marriage, wait for 'Mr Right' to bump into her by accident, or do without marriage—and a good part of our twenties and thirties are spent thinking about it. Will we meet the right person? Can't the right person be found outside an arranged set-up? Are we settling? How do we know someone is right for us? When do we have children? What do we tell our relatives when they ask about 'good news'? What if we can't have children? Will we regret marrying the people we did? Can we study after marriage? What compromises will that involve? How about working after marriage? Is it possible to leave an unhappy marriage? Is having an arranged marriage an admission of defeat, a confession that we simply couldn't find love? Once we're married, does it really make a difference whether it was love or arranged, or do we deal with the same problems and enjoy the same harmony either way?

Each of these questions yielded varied answers, ranging from facetious to poignant. To my surprise, I found that people actually wanted to discuss their marriages, explore their own reasons for getting married, and speak about the little pretences we all hide behind. A friend and I bonded over how, even if we were to have arranged marriages, we wouldn't want people to know it, and would have to think of romantic back-stories—'He saw me at a wedding, and asked his mother's friend to set me up with him'; 'My cousin and she went to the same school, and she was at my aunt's place one day'; 'Our parents are family friends, and we used to play together as kids, apparently, but I don't remember'; 'Both of us were pissed with our parents, and came in with the intention of rejecting each other, and then we realized we'd gone to the same school and had crushes on each other'; and so on.

In writing the stories of the women I spoke to, I grew progressively excited about the book, and it began to evolve beyond its original structure. At times, I would feel I was writing a motivational book, at times a dystopian novel, at times a Barbara Cartlandesque romance. Sometimes, it would appear that arranged marriages, for all the thought that goes into them, are simply wrought by destiny. Just when I was beginning to think there wasn't much difference between a love marriage and an arranged one, one of my interviewees would speak about expectations her in-laws had of her that had taken her aback. Someone else would tell me how, unlike boyfriends, husbands often didn't want to know about their partners' pasts.

However, everyone appeared to feel that there are several levels at which one has to cope in an arranged marriage. There is a lot of pressure on the man too, especially when it comes to mediating conflicts between his wife and his family. Everything in an arranged marriage is a shade different from a love marriage. A bride is seen as conniving, for having got her husband besotted with her. When a couple lives in another town, or abroad, the wife is expected to stay with her in-laws rather than her parents when they visit. Protocol is important. All the women I have spoken to have had challenges to mount, and many had to figure it out for themselves, chiefly because they didn't know people who had shared the experience. Their parents and in-laws, too, have had to deal with certain things.

As the mother of a friend told me, 'Everyone wants sons-in-law like their sons, and daughters-in-law like their daughters. That won't happen. You have to lower your expectations, or at least step back, and let your children take the call.'

This book isn't intended as a guide for women looking to have arranged marriages alone. The women—and men—who have shared their stories and advice are at various stages of that journey. Some are searching for spouses, some have married recently, some have studied after marriage and babies, some have gone to work for the first time after their children began to go to full-day school, some have stuck it out in unhappy marriages and some have walked out of wedlock. Though each story is specific, and though I could glean certain overarching topics and slot them into separate sections, this should perhaps be read as a story of stories—because there was something in each I could relate to, and I hope the reader will feel the same way.

April 2013,
Chennai

'You need to train your man like a dog with potential'

Uttara Singh Chauhan tells us how to romanticize a fiancé and domesticate a husband.

Uttara Singh always knew exactly what she wanted—a television-news anchor, she would work in five channels, for two years each, from ages 20 to 30. She would be married before she turned 25, and spend some quality alone time with her husband. Then, she would have her first child before she turned 30, go on maternity leave, come back, quit, have her second child when her first child was three, and take some years off before figuring out how she would keep herself occupied once both kids were in school.

'I've got it all chalked out,' she would say airily to colleagues, when she was all of 22. Now 28, she's done all of those things, right up to quitting the last channel she worked in. 'Except it was three channels, not five,' she says, somewhat ruefully. 'But maybe I'll do two more before having the next one.'

She also always knew she would have an arranged marriage. She's from a Rajput family, well known in the community, and marrying out of caste, or even out of league, would mean her parents would find it hard to get her older brother married off. Both branches of her family have been in the army for generations, and her mother's only advice to her was to marry out of the army.

'She told me it was a difficult life, and it is,' Uttara says. 'I've seen the things she's had to give up, I've seen how hard it is to carve a home out of a house, and leave it all behind in a year or two, to bring up children all alone, without any help, to keep in mind the rules and etiquette that come with being an army wife.'

So, that was one more thing Uttara knew—she would not marry into the army.

But, despite being armed with a checklist, it wasn't as easy as she'd thought it would be to find a husband. Each candidate was carefully weeded out after having had horoscopes matched, discreet enquiries made, been checked to see if there had been any other alliances between the two families, and made sure the boy was tall, well-educated and 'from a good family'.

Yet, the first time she went to meet a prospective husband, in a coffee shop, she was stunned.

'There was this guy stretching his legs out, and when he saw me, he waved and called out, "Uttara?,"' she recalls. 'Some five people turned and stared. And it was sort of unnecessary because we were on the phone anyway. I put down the phone, and tried to smile. This guy held out his hand . . . *sitting down*. I crossed him off my list.' She knew it would be even easier to convince her parents when he didn't make a move for the bill, but lazily asked, 'How much?' as she reached for it, and paid his share alone.

The next time round, her parents decided to meet the parents of the boy, *and* the boy, before letting him near their daughter. The prospective in-laws were a Business Family. Their business was education. They ran several colleges.

'After a few years of marriage, maybe she can study in one of our medical colleges and become a doctor,' the prospective mother-in-law suggested. 'Then, we can set up a clinic for her, maybe a hospital if our other son also marries a doctor.'

Exit the Singh family.

So, when it was time for them to meet Ranveer Chauhan, they weren't particularly optimistic any more. The families met at Uttara's home.

'There was something nice about him,' she says, 'He didn't check me out, and he didn't turn away. He just stood up, smiled, and said "Hello."'

When her mother asked her to bring the tea, Ranveer's mother stopped her.

'No, no, we've come to talk to you. What's the point of your running around to get the tea when the maids are here?' she said.

After the families spoke for some time, they suggested Uttara and Ranveer head to a coffee shop, chaperoned by her brother. Her brother wasn't sure what to do when they got to the coffee shop, and said, 'Okay, I'll leave you two alone.' Ranveer politely protested, and her brother took him seriously.

'I had to send him a message saying, "Pretend you've got

a phone call,"' Uttara says. 'As soon as his phone beeped, he frowned at it and went, "Hey, I've got a message from you!" So, I had to say, "Must be my other phone. Mama has it. Call her and see what she wants, na?" He clicked on the message, and I said, "Arre, go call her, na?" He finally got it. By then, of course, Ranveer knew exactly what was going on, and it was already awkward. Later, he told me he desperately wanted to laugh, but didn't want to offend me. I sort of wish he had, because that would have cleared some of the tension. As it stands, I don't even remember what we spoke about. I think it was mainly about his work. And he pretended he was really interested in how a news channel works. That's all I remember.'

When her mother asked what she thought, she said she needed more time. Uttara's mother then wanted to know what they'd spoken about, and refused to believe she didn't remember.

But the drama of the day didn't end there. They decided to go shopping at Connaught Place, and suddenly, they saw Ranveer.

'Don't call him,' Uttara hissed, even as her brother shouted out his name.

More awkwardness, as Ranveer walked up and asked them how they were.

'Nothing's changed in the last three hours,' Uttara's brother said.

There was a pause, as they all realized Ranveer had just walked out of a wedding garment store.

'Uh, my friend's getting married,' he said, embarrassed. 'I came to . . . uh, just came along with him.' They all nodded, and he suddenly asked, 'Why don't you come and meet him?' They declined.

'Poor thing, we didn't even know whether he was telling the truth,' Uttara says. It did eventually turn out he was.

Meanwhile, the two families discovered there had been a wedding between the clans already, among close relatives. And Uttara knew there was something she liked about Ranveer. Later, she would say it was his easy manner and his unobtrusive politeness, but the 'something' wasn't any of that—it was that he had taken a few years off from work to look after family land, which was under the care of an aunt who had lost her husband.

'Things like that are important to me. Rajputs are all about land,' she laughs now.

She had no good reason not to marry him, so the family began to make preparations for the engagement. Everyone was rattled. Her mother told her she could break things off if she wasn't comfortable. Her friends told her an arranged marriage didn't make sense, and she shouldn't marry someone she had only met once, especially when she couldn't recall any of the conversation they'd had. She wasn't going to be allowed to meet him between then and the engagement—his family was too conservative, and 'it wouldn't look nice if we asked'.

On the day of the engagement, things got worse.

'So, my best friend went up to him, and looked him straight in the eye, shook his hand, and said, "You're very lucky,"' Uttara said, 'I didn't hear what he said, but she froze. And then, all my friends turned really frigid towards him. That, I discovered later. At the time, I remember closing my eyes, and praying to God, saying, "Please, let me have made the right decision."'

Her best friend was enraged because she thought Ranveer had replied, 'And so is she.' It turned out that she had misheard him, and he had actually said, 'Undoubtedly.' They would find out two years later, when another friend told Ranveer they had all thought he was snooty because he'd made such an ungallant remark. A nonplussed Ranveer would say, 'No, I was so taken aback, I only said "Undoubtedly." I couldn't think of anything more chivalrous to say.' The friend gasped, 'You said, "Undoubtedly"? We all thought you said, "And so is she"!'

But the worst part of the engagement was the photographer, who kept asking them to move closer to each other. Finally, the photographer manually placed Ranveer's hand on Uttara's shoulder. He apologized, and she said, 'It's okay.'

Meeting between the engagement and the wedding was a challenge. He worked in Gurgaon, she in Noida. His timings were 9 a.m. to 7 p.m., hers were 3 p.m. to 11 p.m. Strangely, though, the distance was what showed her she'd made the right decision.

'I remember this one time we were planning to meet around 10 at night. I'd got permission to leave early.' But when she went to the car park, she realized she had a flat. She called up the person in charge of administration, asked permission to leave her car overnight and had a cab arranged. Then, she called Ranveer to tell him she would be delayed.

'He picked up the phone and asked if I'd left, and I said, "Uh, there's a problem, I have a flat tyre." He immediately asked, "Where are you? Are you safe?" And I said, "Yeah, it's the office car park. There's a shuttle that . . ." and he cut in and said, "Okay, get back to office and stay there. I'm coming to pick you up. I'll be there asap." And then he hung up. I had to call him back to say it was all right, I was getting a cab drop, and I could meet him in an hour at my place. But all the way back, I was thinking, he's had a twelve-hour day at work, and he's ready to drive a hundred kilometres to pick up a woman whom he's met just twice. Yes, we were engaged, but it didn't even occur to him to ask whether I could get an office cab. His instinct was to come over and make sure I was safe. Then, I knew.'

Once she knew she'd made the right decision, it was all about making the courtship romantic.

'I had to get him to propose to me,' she says. 'Yes, he'd already given me a ring, and my friends thought I was crazy. But these things are important to me. And it was a very nice ring, so it needed an equally nice story.'

But she wasn't going to ask him outright, because that would kill the romance.

'See, I grew up with dogs,' she says. 'And the thing is, as long as they're intelligent, you can train them. And because they're intelligent, and so satisfied in their intelligence, they won't realize they're being trained. The key is to make them think they're doing what you want them to out of their own accord. So, I decided that was how I needed to look at a man—like a dog with potential.'

It was a week-long project. When they spoke about Hindi movies, she would speak about her favourite proposal scenes. She would compare them to Hollywood films. She would speak about friends of hers, and how their boyfriends had proposed. When she was sure the idea had filtered through, she sighed, 'Sad, na, with an arranged marriage, you don't get to do anything romantic?'

Rajput style, he took up the challenge. 'Why not?'

She got her dream proposal. The wedding didn't go off as smoothly as she would have liked, but more about that in 'The Wedding Hungama'. However, she made sure the ceremony was itself was picture-perfect, as was the bidaai.

'Everyone cried,' she says, 'except this one friend of mine from the south, who was actually moving from Delhi the next day. She was just bewildered by all the crying. Ironically, she was the only one who wouldn't see me for the next year and a half. Everyone else I met as soon as I got back from my honeymoon.'

The mourning turned out to have something of an anticlimax when Uttara and Ranveer returned from their honeymoon to find that the renovation of the flat they were moving into wasn't yet complete. Since his parents lived out of town, they moved in with her parents for a couple of weeks.

'For the first time in my life, my mother was happy looking at my dirty clothes,' she says. 'She was actually smiling when she emptied my suitcase into the washing machine.'

She would use the dog-with-potential theory again, as her first birthday post-marriage neared, and she discovered he wasn't doing anything special.

'See, he's the kind who likes to do a quiet dinner. I'm the kind who needs a surprise party, with nice pictures that someone else will upload on Facebook.'

She called up a friend, and told her to make sure Ranveer

threw her a surprise party, and to make sure he thought it was his idea.

The plan worked like a scene out of *Inception*. Her friend called up Ranveer, and asked when he intended to throw Uttara her surprise party, and whether he needed any help organizing it. She apologized for asking in advance, but explained that Uttara was very sharp, and would figure out what they were up to if he were to start speaking to her friends on the phone more often, or getting connected on Facebook. Ranveer said he would need the numbers of guests he should call.

'He believes he took care of everything, right down to the cake,' Uttara says. 'What can I say, I have good friends!'

Settling into a routine

Once she was married, Uttara had to confront the reality of being mistress of the house. For many women, the shift from their parents' house—where everything is taken care of—to a house that must be run by them can be very hard.

'I actually felt like I was playing House, you know. Like back when we were kids. It was all so funny. For the first time in my life, I was voluntarily getting up before noon, and making coffee for both of us. And seeing him off to work. And interviewing maids, and yelling at them to keep them in their place, and speaking to the ironing guy, and arguing with random people just to play mistress-of-the-house. At some point, I realized I wasn't playing any longer, but it was an easy transition. My advice would be to let it flow. It's incredible how quickly you settle into a routine, and also, that you actually enjoy it. It's nice to build a home, to do little things for each other, to fight over petty things, to work out small agreements. With me and Ranveer, since our work timings were so different, we made sure we woke up for each other. I'd get back around midnight and call him up, though I had the key. He would wake up, come downstairs, open the door and we'd have dinner together.'

Two years and eleven months into their marriage, they had a baby girl. Cuddling the little one, Uttara says, 'I think, somewhere, you just *know* things are right. The most important thing is to go by instinct—can you be yourself with him? Your crazy, insecure self? It's all right to play someone else to his family, to yours, to whatever . . . but you need to be yourself with him. And you need to want to do things for him.'

Star-crossed partners

Vijaya Raghuraman tells us how to beat the horoscope.

It appeared Vijaya Raghuraman and Dileep Shankaran had a lot in common— she was a business journalist, he was an investment banker. She was a trained dancer, he was a trained mridangist. They were both Palakkad Iyers born and raised in Bombay (now Mumbai). And they shared the same nakshatram.

'Our horoscopes didn't match,' Vijaya says, smiling, 'but our hearts did.'

Their story, with a few songs and Manish Malhotra costumes thrown in, could make for a Bollywood romance.

To begin with, Vijaya was engaged to someone else before they met—that, too, had been an arranged match. That betrothal broke because Vijaya's fiancé started having an affair. And it was from the ashes of this alliance that a new one was forged.

Vijaya and Dileep were introduced by the cousin of her ex-fiancé, who was a close friend of Dileep's.

'He was very upset when the engagement broke,' Vijaya recalls, 'and I think he felt guilty, because he's very fond of me, and I'm very close to him. So, he said, let me patch you on to my friend Dileep, and we'll see how things go. Now, here's the second twist—Dileep wanted the horoscopes to match.'

This was because his sister had had a love marriage, out of caste, and he had promised his mother he would (a) only marry an Iyer girl (b) do it with all the traditional trappings, starting with horoscopes.

'How filmy,' I said, when she first told me.

Vijaya grinned. 'You haven't even heard the filmy part.'

The horoscope matching was going to be tricky, because Vijaya was born under the Moola nakshatram, which is considered unlucky for the groom's family. Girls with this star find it hard to get married into families that set store by horoscopes.

'For two years, my parents had looked and looked and looked and looked, and finally the one that broke off happened,' Vijaya laughs. 'So, they didn't really care for horoscopes after that.'

Meanwhile, Dileep's friend told Vijaya's parents about the match.

'Dileep Shankaran?' Her father frowned. 'I know him.'

It turned out that a close friend of her father's had suggested the match a couple of years earlier. But he had said Dileep would only be willing to get married in two years, and they should get in touch with the family around that time. Before the time was up, of course, Vijaya was engaged to someone else.

Now, Dileep's family sent the horoscopes to multiple

astrologers, in the vain hope that at least one would be able to conjure up compatibility.

'The first one said one of us would die. Another person said a divorce is sure to happen,' she says, 'See, Dileep also happens to be born under the Moola nakshatra. And the very first principle of horoscope-matching is you don't take the same nakshatra, because the traits are the same, so you'll end up clashing. Or, if the personalities are not very strong, your life may not be that successful and stuff like that. So, we decided to call it off.'

But, in the meanwhile, Dileep had seen her photograph, got curious about his prospective bride, and looked up her business reports and television show on YouTube and TV. And he'd decided he had to make it work.

'He got in touch with me, saying he had some query about a certain company. I didn't think anything of it. I was a business journalist, he was in investment banking, and we'd already decided the wedding wouldn't happen. So, this was just a favour for an acquaintance.'

However, once they got talking, they didn't stop. They would chat online, or he would call up, and they got to know each other very well.

'One fine day, he said, "I really like you, and I want to give it a shot."' She smiles, saying, 'And he wanted to set up a meeting. I told him, "But you yourself said you're particular about the horoscope, so what do you want to do now?" And he said, "I'm trying to get in touch with a lady my parents have been consulting for the last many years, but I'm unable to reach her right now. Let's see what happens." I said, okay, fine.'

She told her parents what had happened, and that she found

him to be a 'nice guy', and if things worked out with the third astrologer, she would like to meet him and then possibly get married. Her parents were open to it, as long as his family didn't raise an objection.

Meanwhile, Dileep's friend—Vijaya's ex-fiancé's cousin—was giving her live updates on the progress of the horoscope, and the turmoil it was causing Dileep. The third astrologer said there may be some health issues, but there were no complications serious enough to thwart the marriage, though it wasn't the best match.

Vijaya herself doesn't dismiss astrology, though she isn't convinced by the idea of horoscope-matching. 'Astrology is a science, actually, and a lot of people don't realize that. They think it's superstition. But, one of the astrologers we know believes horoscope-matching should not be done. Because by marrying someone, my horoscope is not going to change, my fate is not going to change. What is written is going to happen. It will not become better or worse if I marry someone. So, he refuses to do horoscope-matching.'

The expert opinion was another factor in convincing Dileep he should go ahead and meet Vijaya. By then, a month and a half had passed since he'd got in touch with her and started trying to iron out the hitches in the horoscopes. He was based in Chennai at the time, and had to make a business trip to Mumbai.

'It's funny, our horoscopes didn't match, but destiny made all our decisions,' Vijaya muses, 'First, if the first engagement hadn't happened, I wouldn't have met him through the cousin. And he wouldn't have got curious about me if the cousin hadn't said this girl is really nice, you'll get along well, and all that. And the thing was, my father had actually seen him play the mridangam when he was a child, five or six years old—because my father was very active in the Carnatic music circle in Bombay, my grandfather and great-grandfather were both well-known vainikas. And it turned out my father actually knew Dileep's family very well. Plus, my father's close friend had recommended the match two years before we got in touch. And now, there was this trip. So, there were too many things involved to write it off easily. Probably that's why Dileep also changed his mind about the horoscopes.'

It's a romantic *arranged* marriage tale, and Vijaya is pragmatic in the telling of it. 'We didn't meet up front. We didn't see each other face-to-face till the end. It was not love at first sight or anything like that. It started off like an arranged marriage because it happened very formally, and then the thread broke. In a typical set-up, this would have ended with the horoscopes not matching. But then, all this drama happened, and he was very sure I'm the girl he wanted to marry.' She pauses, and reflects over her life since the wedding. 'It's been quite fun the last two years. We really connect on everything. I think it was a very good decision to overlook all that horoscope stuff.' And she laughs.

The connect

When do you know this is the man for you, that it has actually clicked? Vijaya feels it's an organic process. They would chat every day, for a month or so. And from the sort of things that came up in conversation, from the similarity in their idea of what they wanted from life, the value systems they were raised in, she knew there was something in there. Add to this the fact that they were both Palakkad Iyers raised in Bombay, and had several languages in common.

Knowing the man is right

What made Vijaya so sure Dileep was the right man, especially when she had just come out of a broken engagement? She draws the distinctions between the process the first time round, and with Dileep.

'The first time, I was pressurized for an answer. Yes or no was left to me, but they wanted to know quickly. So, maybe I made an error of judgment there. We didn't get to know each other properly. In the eight months after the engagement, I got to know him better and I realized that there were so many things that didn't match about us. The larger goals may be the same, but as people, we were very different in most ways. He liked to party, go out, eat out . . . he was just too social and outgoing for me.'

She doesn't blame peer pressure—friends getting married all around her—or parental pressure. She sees their point, and measures her words carefully. 'Once I'd met him, my parents just wanted an answer, and they wanted it quickly. I think they regretted that they did that, but they were facing pressure from his father also. He didn't have a mother, and his father was quite an aggressive, dominating character. In fact, the father called me directly, and asked me what my answer was!'

It was complicated because she got along well with

everyone in his family, and is still in touch with some of them. 'I connected very well with them, but somehow I never connected with him. And I was always in denial, I think, about it, till it actually happened. In all fairness, I may not have been able to gauge this even if I'd had more time, but sometimes, when families think *they* connect really well, then they want an answer quickly, and that's not, well, fair. That's why I tell everyone I meet, who's looking out—don't make decisions hastily, and come what may, don't give in to what your parents or his parents want you to do.'

Neither of them could relate to each other, and he started seeing someone on the sly after the engagement.

Things were very different with Dileep because the families were hardly involved. They assumed it had been shelved once the horoscopes were found to be discordant.

With a laugh, she says, 'They thought it was all over, and we'd go find other people. But then we told them we'd met online and chatted and we really liked each other and wanted to meet, and eventually, that we wanted to get married.'

Dileep and she wanted almost exactly the same things. 'Both of us knew that we didn't want the mundane kind of life, just going to work, coming back and crashing. Both of us knew that we wanted to spend time with each other, and with the families. That was of primary importance. We didn't want to work in stressful jobs that keep you cooped up in office all the time. And we wanted to travel as soon as we'd saved some money.'

Despite all this, she says with fond exasperation, 'We fight all the time about one thing, though. I'm very particular about how clean the house must be, and he doesn't give a damn. He leaves things all over the place, and he's really absent-minded, and I have to pick up after him.' She shakes her head.

Living with an artiste

There was something else too—both she and Dileep were keen on his pursuing his musical career. Dileep had taken the 'safe' route, like all good boys. He was something of a prodigy in his teens, accompanying senior musicians on foreign tours. But he gave it up temporarily, to focus on his studies, and then got a job in a multinational company.

However, when he told her he felt like giving up the job to get back to music full-time, Vijaya was very clear on what he should do.

'I told him please go ahead and do it, because this is the only time he'd get, the next two or three years, when he could try it out, and see whether it would work out or not.' It's been a year and a half, and while he's doing quite well now, what he earns doesn't compare with the pay cheque he brought home when he was a full-time investment banker.

'He keeps feeling sad all the time that I'm the one supporting us, while he's trying to secure his career. I have to reassure him all the time, and say, "See, that's not an issue. If I were the one who was sitting at home, you'd never say it, so I don't think you should say that when you're attempting to do something. It's okay, I don't mind going to work and earning money while you're doing this, it's all right."'

He does work part-time as a consultant, and Vijaya points

out that if he does get that break and makes it as a musician, it would have all been worth it.

Moving cities

When her parents started looking out for a groom, Vijaya was adamant that she wouldn't leave Mumbai. However, after meeting Dileep, she was willing to move to Chennai, because that's where he was best placed to build a career in Carnatic music.

'I've actually enjoyed being here, though I miss Mumbai a lot. What I miss about Mumbai most is family—my parents, my in-laws, all our relatives who are in Mumbai. I miss them, and the fact that there's no family support. It can get a bit problematic when he's travelling, when I feel really alone. But there are other advantages—like, we have our own private space. And I don't know whether, in today's world, geography matters that much. Also, Mumbai's become too busy and too crowded, and too chaotic. So, it's not too bad.'

They also got to build a home together. Before marriage, Dileep had stayed in semi-furnished homes, and 1 BHK houses whose décor he didn't care about.

'Sometimes, he would only have a chair and bed,' Vijaya laughs.

But after the engagement, he booked a brand new 3 BHK for them to rent. He decided to shop for a showcase, sofa set, dining table, cots and all the other basics. He would send Vijaya pictures for her approval, before ordering the furniture.

'Even now, when we're planning to shift within the city, he's so enthusiastic about making a home look nice and welcoming. That sort of thing really helps us bond,' she smiles.

The army wife

Shreya Gopal tells us how to mind one's cues and live in peace as an army wife, explains how an inter-caste arranged marriage works, gives us lessons on conflict resolution, and tells us how a herbivore and carnivore can co-habit.

A few months ago, Shreya Gopal was used to the routine of a working woman who had the luxury of living with her parents—she would wake up, make herself breakfast, head to work, come home, watch TV, have dinner, and either sleep or head out with her friends. Since January 2013, she's been the wife of Captain Rajiv Venkatesh, tucked away in an old British cantonment in north India. She spends her day ordering maids about, supervising the cooking, keeping house, telling herself she does need to take a few months off after marriage, and asking her mother—also an army wife—how to deal with the protocol that comes with living in the officers' quarters.

It has been nearly ten years since Shreya was first pulled into the marriage market. And when she finally found the man whom she knew she could spend the rest of her life with, criteria such as caste and ethnicity had been discarded by her family. She's Malayali, he's Tamilian. She'd grown up in army cantonments across the country, and settled down in Chennai. He'd grown up in Delhi, chosen a career in IT, and then quit to join the army.

'But to get to this meeting, there are a lot of horror stories we need to deal with first,' says Shreya.

It all began when she was in her final year of undergraduation. There had been a flurry of weddings in the family, and she would attend most in saris.

'While socializing with relatives, someone would come up and discreetly ask my mother's aunts or someone how old I was, and what I was doing, and whether I was available,' she recalls. When her great-aunts asked to come home and chat over a cup of tea, Shreya initially assumed it was to share the sort of gossip that is regularly stirred up at weddings. Soon, she found out what it meant. There was a "boy"—he could be in the merchant navy, in a reputed software company, in an engineering firm, running his own business; but he was always from a "good" family, he was always the "perfect" match, and he was always God's gift to womankind.

'My maternal grandmother was very disgusted with the whole thing. She was insistent that I get married only after I'd finished my postgraduation and got myself a job. But, of course, everyone would tell her, "No, only if we start looking now will something *right* come along in four years."'

After her graduation, Shreya headed off to Delhi to do a

diploma in Mass Communication, and returned to Chennai to do her Master's in Literature.

'Since I was 21, and it wasn't inappropriate any longer to make enquiries about me, the circus began. People would speak to relatives of relatives, they would speak to aunts, they would speak to my mother, and sometimes they would even speak to me. Finally, my father decided I should start looking, and I was registered with a bunch of shady matchmaking-bureau-type places, and Malayali Associations and whatnot. You know, some of these have a subscription fee, and I seriously lost my temper. Hello, I'm not some cow to be sold off on the marriage market!'

The first couple of years, she rejected every 'expression of interest' that came her way. Finally, there was a boy, 'strongly recommended' by distant relatives. That ended the minute she saw his Frank Zappa moustache. Her interaction with the next prospective groom was over the phone, and she quickly found out they had nothing in common. The third one fell through when he asked if they could share a 'cock', and then pointed at the Coke she was about to sip. A fourth was nipped in the bud when the groom's father noticed that Shreya's arm was folded under her sari in the photograph her parents had sent, and wanted to know whether they were camouflaging a deformity. A fifth came to naught when Shreya and her brother found out the backdrop of an American city had been Photoshopped into the picture of the groom.

'And then, like any good, traditional Malayali father, my dad went through his Dubai phase, where he was finding only boys from the Gulf. See, my father believes everyone from Trichur and Palakkad is nice. My mother's from Trivandrum, and she was like, "No way am I having a son-in-law from Trichur." So, thanks to the internal politics, I was a happy spectator.' Shreya pauses. 'But then it went online. Oh my God. I was registered on every portal. But it got really sidey when I started getting Facebook friend requests from all these morons.'

Meanwhile, the Gulf phase continued. Offers came in from Riyadh and Jeddah. 'I was like, wait, I live in a country where I can wear a T-shirt and shorts, and take an auto or a bus and go to Landmark and buy books for 3000 rupees, all by myself. Maybe I'm one of two girls in this city doing it, but I can. I don't see why I should volunteer to live in a country where I should wear a burqa, and must be accompanied by a man wherever I go.'

The incident that finally put an end to the Gulf phase was a phone call from the father of a prospective groom. He told Shreya's father that they had twenty acres of farmland, and there was no need for Shreya to work. The son was in Dubai, and the parents thought he would save more money if he continued to live alone. 'They said, oh, the two of them can meet once a year. I told my parents I would run away from home if they let those people meet me.'

Finally, Shreya put down three conditions—that a man who wanted a tall, fair, beautiful wife must have, at the very least, a full head of hair; that he should be open-minded; and that he should read. Luckily for her, the family astrologers said she would have a late marriage, according to her horoscope. None of the women on her mother's side of the family, starting with her grandmother, had married under the age of 25. So, her demands for an intellectual match were humoured. However, when her younger cousins began to get married, the search got frantic. No one was worried about caste any longer. Any boy who fit Shreya's conditions would do.

The fit

The way Shreya's family saw it, these were the basics:
* ❖ Good job, preferably an engineer
* ❖ Good family
* ❖ Horoscopes should match
* ❖ Taller than Shreya
* ❖ Decent-looking enough to introduce to people

The rest of it was up to her. She would have to decide what was important, and sort it out with the groom.

'I've had so much independence all my life—I was allowed to choose my course of study, the clothes I wore, how much money I spent, when I came back home . . . the only condition was that I made arrangements to get dropped back safely. And to give up that sort of life, the person has to be really worth it,' Shreya says. And so she put down the conditions.

The conditions

'I think the main thing for me was that he should be open-minded. When you've grown up in a big city, people think of you as "that kind of girl", who drinks and who has had multiple boyfriends, and lots of sex, and who's like this and who's like that. I was very sure that I don't want to spend the rest of my life with someone who is going to use every possible occasion to point out to me that he's done me a favour by overlooking all of these assumptions and presumptions and marrying me,' Shreya says. 'I would rather spend the rest of my life with someone who's open to at least accepting the kind of life that I have led. Because I'm not going to apologize for it. Why should I? I haven't done anything wrong. I haven't lived a sinful, hedonistic life. I've just lived a liberal life. In fact I don't get why people attach labels like "progressive" and "liberal" to it. This is my money, and I've earned it by working sixteen- to eighteen-hour shifts at work. So if I want to spend it on alcohol and partying, that's my right. And, ideally, I would like a man who reads something other than the newspaper, but as long as he's open-minded, everything else is negotiable.'

When she spoke to Rajiv on the phone, their first conversation lasted more than two hours. 'It wasn't like we were having one intellectual epiphany after the other, but it was good conversation. He was sensible and level-headed. And he didn't judge me for going to watch *Veer Zara* in the theatre.' Shreya laughs, 'Well, actually it turned out both of us are Shahrukh Khan fans, and we both think Yash Chopra makes good movies. But most importantly, he didn't have a mould he expected me to fit into. I think we both had pretty much the same criteria for partners—we wanted people who could talk, who would listen, whom we could relate to.'

Their temperaments were alike too. 'Yes, there were disagreements. And yes, inappropriate things were said on both sides, and there were arguments, but those were resolved in a very healthy, sane manner. It's very difficult to come across someone who's willing to do that in a conflict—most people want to prove their point, at the cost of the other person's feelings, and sometimes at the cost of the relationship. He was willing to negotiate through the problems.'

There appeared to be only one hitch—Shreya is vegetarian, Rajiv is not. However, as the only vegetarian in her family, she had had a lifelong exposure to non-vegetarian food and non-vegetarian cooking.

'Of course, I spend a lot of me time bitching and moaning and whining about how it's God-awful, and you've slaughtered animals for this, but it's honestly not such a big deal that I would refuse to eat at the same table,' Shreya says, 'I mean, my family only goes to restaurants with a vast repertoire of non-vegetarian dishes. They eat anything except insects, dog and snake meat, I think. I told him I won't cook meat, because all my reservations about the ethics aside, I don't really see myself cleaning fish, and putting masala in it, and frying it. Sorry, I don't love anybody that much in life. And he was okay with that arrangement.'

The clinching factor

'As much as you want to romanticize things like oh, I have such a perfect relationship, we have such remarkable conversations, we talk for hours and hours and hours, the truth of the matter is that this will not be enough. You need to grow as a person, and you need to grow with him, and because of him, and he has to grow because of you. With Rajiv, I don't find it so hard to admit that I'm wrong. I feel no shame in admitting I'm not perfect either. To apologize, to admit you're wrong, for no ego to come in, it's a lot easier with him.'

But more than anything else, Shreya was heartened that Rajiv understood that she would have to, at least temporarily, give up her career to be with him. He made it a point to tell her this, and to reiterate that the money he made would be *their* money, and she must never feel she had to ask him for it. It would be given to her to handle.

Being the army wife

Though Shreya was an army kid, she wasn't quite prepared for everything that goes with being an army wife. 'At army parties, all the kids are thrown out to entertain ourselves. And there are no formalities, except that you're taught to wish an officer and an officer's wife. But now, there are these formal sit-down dinners, and these parties in which your behaviour is scrutinized.'

With a sigh, Shreya recounts her *Pretty Woman* moment. 'So, at this very proper dinner, I was trying to get at a cherry tomato in my salad with my fork, and it jumped off my plate and across the table . . . and there was this look of absolute horror on my husband's face, like he wanted to bury himself right there. Of course, everyone else at the table was too polite to say anything . . . which made it worse. If someone had made a wisecrack about it, we could have laughed it off, but no.'

As a junior wife, one has to be careful not to get on the wrong side of anyone, because—as most army wives will anonymously testify—the senior wives' inputs to their husbands do influence the careers of young officers. 'If your husband's boss's wife decides that she doesn't like you, it could show in his annual reports.'

Shreya also found she had to pay more attention to sartorial matters than ever before. 'You can't repeat your clothes. You have to watch what you wear. If someone senior is around, you have to wear a salwar-kameez or a sari. Jeans and T-shirts are out of the question when you're this low down in the pecking order. Then, you have to worry about sleeveless and backless. But finally, I put my foot down. Fun facts of life—people will stare, people will talk, people will judge. That is how society is. And you and I are not any different. We comment on people too. Whether I'm wearing a high-backed blouse or a backless blouse, people will have something to say. So, now, I just wear whatever style of blouse I want to.'

She acknowledges that marriage involves a lot of adjustment for the army man too. 'He's not a bachelor any more, so he can't walk into someone else's house and say, "Ma'am, give me food." He can't disown me at a party and wander off to the other end, because people will be watching to see if he's checking up on me or not.'

Can someone who hasn't had any exposure to life in the army fit into this milieu? Shreya says it's all about how one handles oneself. 'The bottom line is you need to be able to do the smiling-and-nodding-and-staying-politically-correct thing really well. You need to be intelligent about it. You can't come into this organization and then bitch about the politics. There is politics, there are other women involved, your husband will not be around to hold your hand through this entire process. But, ultimately, if you're drawn to army officers because you're drawn to men with chivalry, with manners, who look good in uniform, well and good. Just remember it's not the civilian world. You *will* have to be adult about dealing with maids, and dealing with other people. You *will* have to learn how to give instructions, how to be master of the house, you *will* have to learn how to stand on your own two feet, and hold your own with other women, because somebody or the other is going to constantly be trying to bring you down. It *is* a contest, and you have to be smart about it. If you can't handle it, you can't. There are lots of wives who either go back to stay with their parents, or work in some other city, away from their husbands.'

And, importantly, an army wife must be prepared to see very little of her husband at times, because their schedules are non-negotiable. For now, Shreya says she depends on her mother's advice and lessons on how to be a good army wife, without losing her sanity.

A suitable Muslim

Zainab Haider speaks of why she entered an arranged marriage, and the compromises she has had to make to handle a career, children and home.

Zainab Haider was 26 years old, when she began to contemplate marriage. She had grown up in Guwahati, moved to Delhi for college, and got a job as a reporter with a Hindi news channel. She would later move on to anchoring in an English news channel. In that time, she had dated a couple of men, but she quickly realized that she would relate to a Hindu from Assam better than she could to a Muslim from elsewhere.

'There's such a cultural difference,' she says, 'In Assam, people don't carry their religious identity in their outfit or in their personality. You will not be able to make out a Muslim girl from a Hindu girl in Assam. The local culture is more predominant. My mom wears saris and mekhela-chador, the local dress. She's not dressed in the traditional Muslim outfit of salwar-kameez and hijab and all that.'

This total assimilation into the local culture carries over to festivals. She couldn't imagine not celebrating Bihu or Diwali with the same enthusiasm as she did Eid. On the other hand, she found a clear delineation between Hindu festivals and Muslim festivals in the north.

'I'd never thought of the sari as unIslamic, but then, some people do feel that you shouldn't expose your tummy or your back,' she says. 'The profession I'm in, most of the Muslim women I meet come from liberal families, I guess, or they wouldn't be reporting and anchoring at odd hours. But sometimes, when I would visit the homes of certain friends, it would strike me how culturally apart we are, you know. Certain things are expected of you, which I wasn't raised with. They say "salaam alaikum"', and you greet people with the adaab, and we were not taught all that. I don't say "inshallah" and "mashallah" that often.'

She did meet the parents of her boyfriend, and found that they came from a very traditional family. 'His father had a long daadi and a topi, and spoke chaste Urdu. His mother wore the hijab. It's funny how communities are divided by language here. For example, the Assamese word for "sister" is the same, irrespective of what your religion is. Whereas, here, Hindus will say "didi", and Muslims will say "apa" or "baaji". I couldn't imagine adjusting into a family like this. In a Hindu family in Assam, the only difference would be that you would have to wear a sindoor or a bindi—your life wouldn't be any different otherwise. In fact, one of my Muslim friends from Assam had a love marriage with an Assamese Hindu, and I don't see her having any adjustment issues. Sometimes, her husband says the Kalima along with her. When his parents visit, she wears sindoor. It's quite cute, really.'

Since she didn't want to marry out of her religion, and hadn't found anyone she could relate to the way she had wanted, Zainab asked her parents to look out for a suitable boy. Within a week, they found Haider Waheed.

Deciding on an arranged marriage wasn't particularly fashionable. 'I know it seems irrational and unbecoming of a modern girl who's got a Mass Communication degree and appears on television and all that, but I have a very strong sense of intuition, and I've always followed my gut feeling. I don't always go by reasoning, logic, or even social norms. Peer pressure never bothered me, or what people would think. And whether it's to do with the friends I choose, or the decisions I make in life, my intuition has proved right. And my intuition told me that an arranged marriage would work out better than trying to build a marriage with any of the boyfriends I'd had.'

Zainab was very sure that she couldn't live in isolation— family is important to her, and, ideally, she wanted as cordial, casual and pleasant a relationship with her in-laws as she had with her parents. 'My social conditioning was such that I had to gel with the guy's family. It wasn't the guy alone that I was getting married to. If it had been, I could have thought, "Arre, what the heck, anyway, we're going to live elsewhere, what do his parents' clothing and outlook matter?" and settled down with my boyfriend. But these things were ingrained subconsciously, and I can't be one of those girls who break away from family.'

There was also another factor she couldn't relate to. In her

Delhi circle, people tended to speak about money, and even measure their boyfriends in terms of prospects. One of her friends, while advising her on marriage, asked her to make sure her husband made good money. 'She actually said, "No mon, no fun",' Zainab recalls, with a laugh, 'and I was totally shocked. I mean, how does somebody *talk* like that?' It got worse, when a friend told her she was foolish for thinking of getting engaged to a man without knowing how much money he made. 'How can you judge a man based on how much he earns? I was appalled.'

Ironically, for Zainab, it turned out to be the validation of her choice she was looking for. She knew that she couldn't relate to someone who'd grown up with such a materialistic outlook. She wasn't used to discussing money, and she knew that she had made the right choice in deciding to look for someone who shared her background.

Finding the right man

In choosing her partner, Zainab looked at what she describes as 'the entire package.' First up, were his parents. Mr and Mrs Waheed were very liberal. They were well-travelled, modern and highly educated.

'Back in the seventies, they had been to Europe, when most Indians hardly left their own states to go and work, you know,' she says. 'And my mother-in-law is a postgraduate. I knew that if you have education and exposure, chances are that you will not be narrow-minded. And Haider's parents have a very expansive worldview. I could see myself fitting into the family.

I knew they would not impose all sorts of restrictions on me.'

Once that was out of the way, she went by her instinct with Haider.

'I knew right away that this was a great guy,' she says, 'He struck me as dependable. I could imagine him being the father of my kids. And the first time we met, we didn't run out of conversation at all. Even now, we can discuss anything, from something on BBC Entertainment, crime and politics, or the Metro construction, to what the children are going through in school, and our investments.'

Making marriage work

Zainab sees marriage as a partnership of two people, and compares it to running a corporate. It takes monitoring. It takes work. It takes effort and willingness to sort out problems.

'See, for a company to run like a well-oiled machine, you have different departments—HR, logistics, finance, sales. And the same thing holds in a marriage. I'm not talking about dividing up chores here. I think a marriage has to work on several levels.'

She identifies five parameters in order to ensure that a partnership is healthy and successful:

❖ Love
❖ Trust
❖ Respect
❖ Intimacy
❖ Friendship

Just as not all departments in a company function at full steam, not all these five will necessarily touch an optimum.

'The first thing people need to understand about marriage is that you can't tick everything off a wish list. It isn't going to be perfect. But there has to be enough there for you to want to make it work. If none of these factors are there, you know the marriage is not working. However, as long as some are there, you work on the rest. Some people may stay together because a good sex life is enough. Some people stay together because they love each other—maybe there's been infidelity, and the trust is gone, but they can't live without each other.'

Speaking of her own marriage, Zainab says trust, respect and friendship are the most important elements to her. When those three factors are working, the others follow anyway. And though there are six years between her and Haider, the fact that they can speak to each other about anything in the world gives their relationship a special bond.

'These are things one has to work on constantly. Love will grow in a marriage, but that's not enough to keep things together. People speak about compatibility. What they mean, I think, is the ability to share anything, to strike a certain comfort level. You should be able to talk to your spouse as you would talk to a friend. Sometimes, very unlikely friendships are struck because of that sense of a comfort level. And that same element is very important in a marriage.'

She believes that even if one of these five elements fails, the relationship suffers. So, the couple—and more importantly, the woman—needs to work on all these elements.

'Whatever you say about the modern woman, the

coordination at home is her department,' Zainab laughs. 'You establish the rules of the house, and you need to make sure your relationship is working.'

Rules for a relationship

One of the most important aspects of a relationship, says Zainab, is transparency. Unless there is trust and honesty, and a willingness on the part of both the man and woman to open up, a marriage will not work.

'Even when you meet someone for the first time, you can gauge whether he's the kind who's uptight and closed,' she says. 'If you know he won't let his defences down, if he won't open himself up, there's no point in pursuing it. Outside relationships, people who are guarded about their lives are your acquaintances, not your friends. To me, friendship is more important than all the frills—right religion, right salary, right height, right prospects, right education, all that is fine. But if he's built a fortress around himself, he's not going to be a friend. And I think friendship has to extend to a husband-wife relationship also.'

After marriage, Zainab made one important rule. They would not go to bed angry with each other, no matter how big a fight they had had during the day.

'Of course, there will be fights,' she says. 'Living with someone, dealing with each other's idiosyncrasies, and sharing personal space leads to arguments, sometimes ugly ones. But whatever problems we've had through the day, we work them out by the end. At the end of the day, I need to be in his arms, knowing this is where I belong, and everything is right with the world. Then I feel secure, like nothing else in the world matters to me. I would be miserable if I cried myself to sleep. So, I make sure I never do.'

Balancing a marriage, career and children

Zainab, now a mother of two, feels the first hurdle a woman needs to overcome while getting into marriage is the mental block. 'There are a lot of girls in my office who say they'll give up working after marriage. And the married ones who are working plan to give up work after having children. Because their attitude is, "Kaise karoongi? How will I manage?" You've already created those demons in your head. But let me tell you, the fear is always bigger in the mind. The real problem is far easier to sort out, as long as you stay pragmatic.'

When Zainab and Haider got married, he was posted in Guwahati, and would stay there for three years. She had to move back from Delhi. They weren't sure where he would be posted next.

'Now, most people want to spend a couple of years on an extended honeymoon—hanging out together, travelling the world, just having fun without any responsibility,' she says. 'But I wanted to have kids. And I knew that it would be easier in Guwahati, with both sets of parents around. I could take up a job, so that my résumé wouldn't show a gap, and when we moved, the child would be a year and a half old, so I could leave him or her with the maid for a short time, and get back to serious work. Waiting for two years would mean I would have to take another break from work to have a baby, and I may not have the same level of support.'

She knew she was missing out on the fun she could have had, but she didn't want to give up her career for marriage. So, she had her first child within a year and a half of her marriage.

'If you're going to balance being a wife, mother and a working woman, you need to plan. I had my baby at 29, and I only went on maternity leave, because my mother was right there. So I went back to work in Guwahati, and when we moved to Delhi again, my daughter was a year and a half old, just like I'd wanted.'

Once she got back to Delhi media, she knew that she wouldn't be able to handle the strain of reporting. And so, she chose to anchor news instead. She was given an early morning slot. This meant she worked unearthly hours—3 a.m. to 10 a.m. But she got to spend most of the day with her baby. By the time she was asked to do afternoon and evening news slots, her child was in playschool.

'I believe that life helps you adjust, things work themselves out,' Zainab says. 'You need to stay positive and optimistic, and things fall in place. Don't panic that your entire life has changed, because it will mould itself to you, or you will mould yourself to it.'

A few years later, Haider came across a big job opportunity. This would involve moving back to Guwahati, and Zainab wasn't sure she wanted to give up everything she had worked so hard for. They had just bought a pretty flat, and she had spent months doing it up. She was poised to grow in her career. But she was in her early thirties, and her child was four years old, and it was time they started thinking about having a second child.

'It was a hard decision. This time, I would have to actually quit my job, because I couldn't work out of a bureau. Guwahati isn't a metro, and my channel already had one correspondent for the northeast.'

She went back, and duly had a son. But she wasn't completely happy being a mother and wife, and nothing else.

Her friends from media had progressed in their careers, and she had taken a break. Many of them were unmarried, and most had no children. She had already done what they planned to do in the next five years. She could catch up with them, eventually. It made sense logically, but Zainab was anxious and restless. There *were* journalists who'd done it all. A few years ago, at 2 p.m., she'd been adlibbing as the Left front walked out of UPA I. Now, at 2 p.m., she was waiting for her daughter to come back from school and monitoring her son's feeds.

To get back to her career, Zainab would have to go to a big city again. It didn't make sense for her to stay in Guwahati. It didn't make sense for Haider to leave. It was the sort of situation that could easily have led to resentment on her part, and soured a marriage that was working well.

'And this is where respect comes in,' she says, 'I spoke to him about the situation, and he was all right with my moving to Delhi with the kids, while he looked for a job that was good enough for him to come back. In the meanwhile, he'd visit us once or twice a month. And that's what keeps our marriage working—he respects my space, my decisions equally, and so we're partners in the true sense.'

She's aware that if he's not able to find a vacancy at his level, she may have to move back, or move to another city. And it will be her turn to accommodate his needs.

'He's been away from the kids for a long time. And you do need to make compromises on both sides,' she says.

When he visits, she allows him to pamper the children, leaving her to play bad cop. This is only one of the many challenges of having to keep a home running and job going, without one's partner around. But every time she feels she has bitten off more than she can chew, Zainab draws inspiration from her maid.

'Not only does she run her own household, but she does the same work in my house, and I wonder how she does it. She's got two kids who go to school to top it all off, and she takes care of mine when I'm not here,' Zainab says. 'I think she's far more efficient and competent as a working woman as I am. I am incapable of running my own household without her help, and here she is, running two!'

Of course, there will be times when every woman who's trying to be the perfect wife, mother and worker will want to shut herself up in the loo and cry. But, Zainab says, every time you're overwhelmed, or feel that you're failing, you need to remember that every woman trying to juggle three roles goes through the same thing. There will always be people who seem to have it more together than you do, but chances are that they have their own problems too.

In a new country

Meera Anthony speaks about how she overcame the problems she faced while moving to a new country, where she wasn't allowed to work for some time.

When Meera Anthony came across Arnav Joseph's profile on a matrimonial site, she had already turned down several men who wanted to know what her hobbies were.

'I found most men I met online irritating,' she says. 'See, I was no good at finding a good guy by myself. Even the short-term boyfriends I had, I would always find a way to end things with them because I'd get bored or irritated soon. My mother was really scared I wouldn't find anyone. But meeting guys for the sole purpose of getting married was a nightmare for me. First, you've narrowed your search down to caste—in my case, Catholic Chettiar. And they would all ask me stuff that made it worse. Arnav was the first who saw the person in me. Never once did he talk to me like he was interviewing me for a wife-job, if you know what I mean. I knew he was different when he looked through my Flickr pictures, and commented on how much he liked the artistic side of me.'

Their conversation was easy and natural, and Meera credits it to what she calls 'Arnav's refined approach'. They would talk about things they liked, their perspectives on just about everything. They met online regularly, got to know each other well, and after chatting for a few months, she agreed to meet him in person.

'We told each other clearly that agreeing to meet didn't mean we were saying yes already,' she laughs. However, they decided not to bother with horoscopes. At the time, Meera was keen for things to work out. Her big concern was that the vision she had in mind, the man, his habits, his demeanour, should correspond to what Arnav really was.

'Even before we met in person, I really liked him and really wanted him to like me back as well. But I wanted to meet him in person just to make sure the reality matched the picture I had of him in my head.' Then, she clarifies, 'When I say picture, it's not just the way he looked, but the way he carried himself, his manners, behaviour and attitude in general.'

The first time they met, they hit it off, and decided to meet again. Their second date-of-sorts was at Juhu Beach. In total filmy style, that was when Meera *knew*. 'It hit me suddenly that this is it. I don't even remember how or why or what it was.'

She was waiting for him to ask her what her decision was, but he didn't. At home, though, their parents virtually had their phones in hand, ready to call each other up and start making the arrangements. And this was when this strange melange of arranged-set-up-love-match became an 'arranged-arranged' marriage, Meera says.

'The first thing I did when I heard he said yes was to call him,' she says. The conversation went something like this.

Meera: You *are* aware that we are getting engaged next week, right?

Arnav: Yes.

Meera: Don't you have to ask me first?

Arnav: Why?

Meera: That's what every girl expects, na?

Arnav: What's there to ask? I knew you liked me.

Three years into their marriage, she says she still holds a grudge against him for not 'asking' her. But every time she brings it up—and she does pretty often—he laughs it off.

And from that moment, there was no time to think. They were engaged and married, then they hopped over to Kashmir for a week-long honeymoon, came back to Mumbai, went to Paris, where her parents live, spent a few days there, and then headed off to Tampa, to start their life together.

Never at any point did Meera have cold feet. She knew he was right for her, and she found the prospect of marriage exciting, not scary or nerve-wracking.

'I remember holding his hand in the plane and thinking 'This is gonna be great.' And I was right . . . I feel that way even now. This *is* gonna be great.'

Building chemistry, building trust

They met quite often, even as their families threw themselves into wedding planning. Arnav was the shy one. Meera says she felt sorry for him, because a fortnight before the wedding, he hesitantly gave her a peck on the cheek. She assumed he'd never dated before.

They had decided not to discuss past relationships. She told him she didn't care about the past, as long as he intended to live in the present, and be faithful.

'Knowing about the past doesn't do any good. It only gives you more reason to worry, especially before a wedding,' she feels.

But with marriage came trust, and they sat down for a full disclosure about ten months into the wedding, when they knew they were comfortable enough with each other not to get paranoid. It turned out they had both dated other people.

'I, for one, didn't want to know their names or any other details because I knew I'd get obsessed about it and ask more questions—and it might irritate him more that I bring up his past. I don't want to be that person. If it's his past, it's his past, and there's no point bringing it up every now and then. I'm his present and that's all really matters to me, I guess.'

She did have one question, though. Why was he so shy before they were married? He shrugged and said he had no idea.

The post-marriage pressures

To most people, marriage marks the day in one's life when one can heave a sigh of relief, certain that no nosy relative can tut-tut, 'It would be nice if you were to get married . . .' or demand, 'When are you getting married? What are you waiting for?' or declare, 'Marriage is all about compromise. You just get into it and make it work.'

Most married people believe a wedding marks the start of new pressures. Just when a couple is waiting to hang out, travel the world and spend alone time together, relatives begin to loom over their heads, pointing at body-clocks and whimpering about great-grandchildren.

'The very next day, we got a full-on lecture from his parents,' Meera says, 'about how we're not getting any younger, and how we shouldn't put off the baby. We just nodded. Honestly, I've never cared for what other people want for me. But since the pressure is from the in-laws and I don't want to be disrespectful, I just nod along and say "All right, no problem". After a while, they stopped pestering us.'

In her case, there was a more telling pressure—finding something to do in a new country, where she did not have permission to work just yet. She didn't want to be home and play housewife, and she didn't want to wait to move until the permits came through.

The big move

Meera had to stay at home for about a year and a half before she could start working, with her Employment Authorizing

46

Document. She knew she would go insane, and so she got busy within four months of living in the United States by working for companies for free. It helped build experience on her résumé, and prevented a gap in her work experience. It would indicate to prospective employers that she wasn't the kind to idle away her time.

Being a web designer, she had to keep in touch with evolutions in design and coding, and she took to studying trends to keep herself up to date.

'Even the few months that I stayed at home, I'd keep myself busy by cooking, learning new recipes, baking and giving baking lessons to my friends. I think Arnav appreciated that about me, the fact that I could keep myself busy without bugging him all the time,' she laughs.

It helped that Arnav already had a large circle of friends. Meera quickly befriended them and their wives. Now, they're a comfortable group that hangs out almost every weekend. They're family to each other, looking out for their own in the absence of relatives. Soon, as she started meeting people in the neighbourhood, Meera made friends of her own.

However, she admits it can be tough, and one should be prepared.

'Sure, there were times when I would break down in front of him, crying that I miss my parents and my brother, and how I hate working my ass off and not getting paid. He was always such a good listener and always said that things would work out, I just needed to have patience,' she says, fondly. 'One of his regular sayings is, "Things always work out in the end; if they haven't worked out, it's not the end." I love that positivity.'

In some ways, it was easier for her to deal with the move to the US, because she had been through a similar shift already, when her family left India to settle in Paris. She remembers vividly the mix of excitement, nostalgia and overwhelming fear at the prospect of leaving India, the country she grew up in, forever.

The shift to the US was easier, because it came without the challenge of a new language, and this made her far less apprehensive than the idea of moving to France had. She had also visited America earlier, and found herself thinking of her immigration as the beginning of another new adventure.

She does feel low at times, since she's not allowed to leave the country except in case of an emergency—one of the mandates as her husband waits on his green card, and she waits on her H1B visa. Her parents and in-laws do visit as often as they can. But she still misses coming to India, where her extended family and most of her friends live.

The hiccups

It's said that if you've got through the first year of a marriage, you can get through anything. As strangers become partners, and begin to share the same spaces, they discover things about each other they hadn't expected. A towel dropped carelessly on the floor, a double-dipped spoon, a clash of favourite TV programmes—just about anything can lead to a fight. Meera didn't find the first year tough in that sense.

'I've heard friends say they would fight about everything—even things as trivial as choosing furniture, or figuring out who cooks when—and they would stop talking for days on end! We've had our silly fights too, but nothing ever serious enough to start a cold war. We talk about it, and have it out then and there.'

But they do have different approaches to the 'having it out'. 'If I'm upset about something, I say that I'm upset, and don't let go until he says he's sorry, and has calmed me down. When he'd get upset, he would just become quiet, and it would show on his face, and I'd start wondering what I did wrong. After making me break my head over it for a while, he'd come and talk to me, and we'd clear things up.'

She feels it's all about egos. Especially in the first year, as one is adjusting to a new presence, it's important to remember that the relationship is more important than the petty issue you're fighting about—that puts everything in perspective, she feels.

From the artiste's eye: staying in tandem

Akhila Ravi tells us how she pursues a career in dance and music after marriage, and what the challenges in marrying an American-raised Indian are.

An arranged marriage may be easy enough for the regular girl with a regular job. But what if you don't fit into the staple mould? What if you're a writer, dancer, painter or musician? Often, women who have taken up these professions feel they're not suited to arranged marriage, especially not with a man who doesn't belong to the same field. However, there are some who believe it can work.

Akhila Ravi, 32, a trained singer who lived in Madras (now Chennai) for most of her life, says, 'I didn't really have an arranged match in the true sense. I sort of arranged it myself.' She had been friends with her now-husband for more than two years, before she realized they would be good for each other, 'at least on paper'. She told him as much, and soon enough, they were married. She hadn't considered going through the traditional routes—ads in the newspaper, matrimonial websites, 'a known family' and the works—because, at the time, she wasn't particularly interested in being married at all.

What changed her mind, then, and how does a woman know when someone is right for her?

Akhila's reply is pragmatic. 'I don't believe that there is such a thing as a perfect match. I think that you can find a mostly good match, but have to work to make it perfect or close to it. People are constantly maturing and changing, within a relationship and outside of it, so being a match is never something that can be taken for granted. In my case, it was really important for me to retain my individuality after marriage. Being able to openly communicate my opinions and feelings without fear of being judged was another. I was lucky enough to find both in one person.'

Anand is a Kannadiga who was born and raised in the US, and so Akhila moved to Texas after marriage. They have now been married for over seven years.

The dynamic in a relationship is, naturally, completely different from friendship. You tell your friends things you wouldn't tell a partner. You hide things from them that you can't hide from a partner.

But Akhila didn't find it awkward. 'I cannot speak for everyone, but for me the transition was fairly seamless as far as accepting a friend for my partner,' she says. 'I've always maintained that it is important to have a friendship, even in a romantic relationship. I believe this makes it easier to be honest and respectful and helps close the distance between two people.'

However, deciding that you may get along with someone is the easy part. Marriage isn't a cakewalk. 'You only really know someone when you begin living with them, so we definitely had our share of adjustments in the first three to four years. Not only because we both grew up completely differently, but also as individuals.'

She says there are four important things a woman must be keep in mind before entering wedlock:

* ❖ Adjustment within reason is crucial to make a marriage work
* ❖ You must have the ability to both communicate and listen
* ❖ You need to understand that the other person will respect you only if you have respect for yourself
* ❖ Aside from your life with your partner, you should also have a life for yourself as an individual

The last, she feels, is most important. 'You need your own activities, your own friends—essentially space from the other person.'

In the years that she has been married, not only did Akhila end up giving Carnatic music performances far more often than she had earlier, but she also began to learn Bharatanatyam. Akhila says she hadn't pursued music with the intention of performing, but a supportive spouse and family encouraged her to.

She doesn't underestimate the importance of a supportive family for an artiste to pursue her interests post-marriage. 'It is definitely very relevant,' she says, when I ask if the idea of needing support is outdated, since women don't really need 'permission' to do what they want to any longer. 'For an artiste to be able to put out their best work, a positive frame of mind and a nurturing environment are essential. If one has to combat an unsupportive family, I think that would definitely hinder the artiste or performer.'

There are several stories of famous musicians having had to battle opposition to their careers. This could range from an angry husband creating a scene at a concert, to parents-in-law—or even parents—refusing to look after the children when the artiste is at practice, or holding a concert. If you're serious about your career in the arts, it is important to pick a man—and a family—that is understanding and encouraging.

Akhila says pursuing her training from the US wasn't too hard. She takes Skype lessons for music, and practises two to three times a week. When she visits India, which is about once a year, she goes to her guru and continues lessons in person.

For dance, she attends classes thrice a week, and sets aside time to practise by herself thrice a week. Though she has to train more rigorously, to make up for lost time, since she got started relatively late, she doesn't see living in the US as a problem. More importantly, visiting artistes from India do hold workshops, and she makes it a point to attend them when possible.

Though Akhila admits that she misses the cultural atmosphere of her hometown, living in the US hasn't hindered her pursuit of the arts. In fact, she began her Bharatanatyam training only in the US, in 2007. 'Since I had never attended a dance class in India, I don't have the benefit of comparison, but I have had a very fulfilling time training in the art form under a wonderful guru who gives me multiple—and frequent—opportunities to perform. Since we do have visiting Indian artistes, I get to attend performances, though perhaps not with the same regularity. It was initially a challenge for me to not have company that was interested in the classical Indian arts, but that's changed.'

While Anand isn't involved in the classical arts, he does enjoy music and dance, and that's good enough. 'He is always a willing audience member at events I perform in, and performances I like to attend. I think it's okay if both people are not into the same things, but it is important for each to respect the other's preferences and be supportive or, at the very least, not be a hindrance,' Akhila says.

Moving abroad after marriage

Since Akhila married a US citizen, and the immigration procedure made it necessary for her to marry in the US, her green card came through without much hassle. But she did have to spend a few months at home, since visa regulations wouldn't allow her to work. 'Those months were quite difficult to deal with, since one is also fighting feelings of loneliness, missing the family you grew up with, adjusting to life in a new country with a fairly new person and so on,' she says.

Having lived in the US for seven and a half years, she says there are lots of opportunities to be had, and feels women shouldn't be daunted by the idea of moving abroad after marriage.

She has some tips for women who will be settling down in another country:

❖ Be open-minded
❖ Be aware that you will be mostly responsible for making the experience good for yourself
❖ Think of a friends' circle beyond your own ethnic community
❖ Take the initiative to go out, meet people and make friends
❖ Even in a position where it isn't possible for you to be gainfully employed, taking up volunteer work and getting out of the house even for a few hours a week does wonders for your self-worth

'What I have enjoyed most about life in the US is the opportunity to meet and interact with people from so many varied cultural backgrounds, and the personal space that you choose whether you'd like to share, or not. I think being open in this regard has greatly aided the success of my marriage,' Akhila says.

When it comes to marrying someone who was raised abroad, an 'NRI' as we term Non-Resident Indians, Akhila warns that the comparison isn't as straightforward as one would think. Just as there is no one 'Indian' mentality, there is no single 'NRI' mentality.

'I've met conservative people, not just men, both raised in India and abroad. Often, since the parents left India in the sixties or seventies, their children are brought up in that perspective—the mentality of that period. Unless they are regular visitors to India, and have kept up with social changes here, they are in some ways more narrow in their opinion of what it means to be Indian and what's acceptable Indian behaviour. It is usually a bit of a struggle between their American and Indian selves.'

She points out that, on the other hand, there are Indian American men who are very broadminded and open. But she adds, 'Although I think sometimes their own opinions might be eclipsed by those of the previous generation, especially if they are living under the same roof.'

Ultimately, it all boils down to the two people in the relationship.

'Even though I knew my husband as a friend, there are some parts of him that are completely American and will probably never change, and I don't necessarily want them to—for example, being able to say no when something is an inconvenience, or not feeling obliged to attend a function merely because it is hosted by a relative. At the same time, he is quite open to my Indianizing him—in the sense that he willingly accompanies me to performances, participates in pujas, loves watching Tamil films and so on.'

Akhila feels that in today's context the definition of what is 'Indian' becomes problematic too. 'We certainly don't have a single national character to speak of, in my opinion—in the sense that most Indians think of themselves in terms of their regional identity, or community-specific identity, first, and only then in the larger sense of 'Indians'. I love the heritage and the arts, and growing up in a family that was so much in support of these things certainly helped shape me as a person, but other than that, I'm not sure how Indian I really am—I find that I am in disagreement with Indian social conventions, especially with regard to women's roles, most of the time. I am sure that anyone with the benefit of a broadminded upbringing such as mine would feel the same.'

So, again, it boils down to not shutting oneself off from a new experience and being willing to make adjustments. 'I guess the sum of it is, if you go into a cross-cultural relationship with an open mind, and not get caught up in the differences, you will probably get the best of both worlds,' Akhila says.

From the artiste's eye: scripting a successful marriage

Ruhani Kapoor tells us why she would have gone crazy if she had married a fellow-writer, and how one deals with temptations outside of marriage.

Writer and poet Ruhani Kapoor met Saadhil Khosla through relatives. They happened to be in the same town at the same time, it was suggested they meet, and soon they were married and settled in New York. Both were in their early twenties, and each worked in completely different industries. Ruhani had a day job in marketing, and moonlighted as an RJ and writer until she had published enough books to confidently quit her office job. She had always known her passion was in writing. Saadhil was in the software industry, and has stayed in it.

One of the most frightening things about being an artiste is the fits of depression most people with a creative bent are prone to. At these times, it's easy to feel alone, and the slightest problem appears magnified. Often, they reach out to fellow-artistes, who not only understand, but empathize. Ideally, one would want to reach out to a partner. Did it worry Ruhani that things may not work out with someone who wasn't from the same field, or from any creative field, for that matter?

'I am always amazed when people marry from within the same field because that would have driven me nuts,' she says. 'I love the fact that my husband uses his left brain and I use the right side. And that we have no overlap in our work. No competition! Jokes aside, I like stability in my life. For a writer, self-awareness is a curse that never leaves you. Gosh, I cannot be with someone whose temperament is similar to mine. It would be chaotic and lethal!'

Referring to her artistic temperament as her 'neuroses', Ruhani says her life choices are driven mostly by emotions. On the other hand, her husband is pragmatic and level-headed—qualities she can't comprehend fully but admires. And the difference in their personalities is a factor each respects.

'There is so much mutual respect, apart from affection. But more importantly, we have never tried to manipulate the other person into becoming who we are. We allow each other room to flourish.'

But, however understanding and compatible one's husband is, there are things in a writer's—or any artiste's—life that someone from another field cannot possibly understand. Take, for example, a writer's block, or her little 'OCDs'—like needing a specific notebook or pen to put something down. Surely this can lead to pangs of frustration?

Ruhani's answer is unequivocal. 'Not at all. What are friends for? Not just for wine drinking and gossiping, you know!'

She recalls that Saadhil once said to her, 'You fulfil all of *my* emotional needs. But I understand that you are an artiste and your emotional evolution is at a pace that I can't always understand, even if I try. I feel happy that you have writer friends and support—people who understand the depth of what you deal with.'

A lot of her writing involves social issues, and Ruhani says that takes her to dark places, both physically and emotionally. 'My husband is always there, making sure I don't drown in those sorrows. Frankly, that's what I need. I don't need another dramatic person sobbing and savouring misery with me. Saadhil might not understand or relate to my 'artistic moments', as they were, but he tries, and lets me be.'

The 'letting me be' factor is something Ruhani treasures. There are times when she wants—needs—be alone. And we're not talking about just solitary vacations. This could happen at a social gathering. It could happen even when they have houseguests. 'Saadhil gets my need for this alone time, to allow my thoughts to percolate. When I disappear inside a bathroom with a notebook, he covers for me,' she laughs. And she couldn't bear to be in the sort of relationship where both partners are prone to emotional rollercoaster rides.

How did she know Saadhil was right for her?

With a grin, she answers, 'Do not drink when you make this decision.' But she doesn't evade the question. 'Problem is, people think too much or just don't think. Just because someone is right—or compatible—with you today doesn't mean that he will be best-suited for you five years from tomorrow. The reality is that we live in a very high-pressure world where tolerance is diminishing every day. And there are distractions surrounding us all. But if your relationship is strong, you can weather anything out.'

Ruhani feels it's possible for any couple to grow apart over the space of a few years. People constantly evolve, and there's only so much one can figure out about oneself and one's partner at any given point. 'Just when you think you've hit the jackpot, people change. There are no guarantees when it comes to love—the biggest myth and mystique.'

Ruhani and Saadhil have known each other for fifteen years, and she acknowledges that both of them have changed in this time. 'It is very easy not to see eye to eye and allow distance to creep in. I have seen very close friends of ours get divorced inside three years of marriage. And also friends whose marriages lasted for ten years. The idea is to evolve, or at least try to, at a similar pace. Or make room for the differences.'

In this context, she believes it's important to 'manage your expectations'. People need to understand that their spouses will not be the answer to all their needs and requirements—and that's okay. And, they need to remember that every new relationship will become old some day; and that any relationship will lack *something*.

But people considering arranged marriage are often apprehensive of exactly who they are marrying. A man—or woman—may not really be what they seem to be. We know we're under scrutiny, and our instinct is to put our best foot forward. Even when the couple has a long engagement, the relationship is in fast-forward mode, possibly because there is a sense of certainty about its outcome. Our partners in arranged marriages don't know what makes us cry, what makes us angry and whether we're prone to fits of madness—things that are bound to come out in a relationship. What if you find out the man you married is not the man you thought you were marrying?

'You'll feel betrayed but you'll get over it. Such is life,' Ruhani answers. 'Because it's not just the guy—you will change too. And it's not just the woman, the guy feels the jitters too. There is no guarantee, irrespective of how you meet your partner, that they will remain the same always. Even while dating, you spend a few hours every day with the guy. It's easy to put the 'best foot' forward. Living with someone under the same roof is a whole different ball game. Instead of focusing on the jitteriness of "how we met", the question should be "How can we be together in a healthy way where we build a good life despite our idiosyncrasies and nuances?"'

Ruhani doesn't rule out the possibility of falling in love with someone else after marriage. However, she points out that this can happen in both love and arranged marriages. As people change, their needs change too, and their partners don't always have the time to notice or listen. 'With both men and women working and leading stressful lives, there will be vulnerable moments. If a situation of the sort arises, first try to identify the problem in your existing relationship. Maybe, just maybe, what you're seeking outside is what's lacking in your real life, your marriage. Do not fear introspection or keeping the lines of communication open with your spouse.'

'As an artiste, given our soaring passion and raging hormones, the probability of finding love multiple times is even higher. Do I recommend extramarital affairs? *No*. But I will also say that we all have one life to live and neither party should feel stifled, ever. As human beings, don't two people owe happiness and respect to each other and themselves? By pretending to be this "happy couple" for the society, we do a disservice to everyone. Imagine walking around your own house on eggshells. Imagine coming back to an unhappy spouse. Imagine drinking tears along with your morning cup of tea or coffee.'

It may be the case that two people are simply not meant for each other, that they married for the wrong reasons. But, Ruhani points out, sometimes a relationship wilts because no one has worked at pulling it out of the rut. On the other hand, 'Sometimes there is no anger or resentment. People just grow apart. It sucks, but it's that way. Sometimes two people don't evolve emotionally at the same pace—it's no one's fault—we all mature at different times. People change and that's a fact of life. All break-ups don't stem from hatred or infidelity or sexual abuse.'

While the older generation is bound to say one must 'adjust' in a marriage, and that marriage is all about compromise, that doesn't cut ice with the modern woman. However, there are two ways to deal with the problems that crop up in a marriage—one may put everything on the table, which *can* prevent misunderstanding, but which may lead to the partner thinking one is nitpicking; or, one may choose what to brush under the carpet, especially if one is given to overanalysis.

'My honesty is my biggest curse,' says Ruhani, with a smile.

'I cannot pretend, so I will share the smallest things that irk me. In my humble opinion, dishonesty catches up with couples and becomes one of the key reasons for any relationship's downfall. Having said that, each couple should figure out their dynamics—not everybody can deal with the truth all the time.'

For an educated, intelligent, working woman who is considering an arranged marriage, Ruhani has one big tip: 'Don't judge yourself. Be kinder. As in, don't doubt your drive or ambition and desire to want it all. If you aren't self-apologetic, life will be easier.'

According to her, our society trains women to send mixed signals and get entangled in a web of expectations that is often of our own manufacture. She points out that not every man wants to be 'served' and treated like a king. 'Many seek equals, you know, and desire for their wives to be more than arm candy. Everyone has their own criteria but my two cents—be with someone who loves you for who you are, not who they want you to be.'

One of the mistakes Indian parents make, she feels, is that they never tell us how much hard work goes into relationships. 'I would also blame Yash Chopra movies for this because life, according to him, is spent romancing in the hills of Switzerland in chiffon saris.' Turning serious, she says, 'It's not easy to constantly think of another person all the time. And to put his needs ahead of yours if you've been an independent woman. Marriage is work. Marriage requires as much attention as a full-time job. Equal, if not more, nurturing. All that took me by surprise.'

However, one can never take things for granted, and it is this realization that ensured that Ruhani and Saadhil have stayed together for so long. 'We both cherish each other's presence and feel grateful for it every day. But neither of us gets complacent or takes our lives or togetherness as a given. I never wake up thinking I will take my husband for granted because he will be around forever. *No*. Never. Being complacent can lead to a slippery slope.'

Peeling off the gloss

Sara Jacob tells us about her checklist, the very unglamorous realities of marriage, and the test her marriage was put through even in its first year.

Sara Jacob, now 29, was used to looking out for herself. Raised in Kuwait, she moved to India to do her under graduation. She headed off to England to do a Master's degree, and when she returned, at 23, the questions began.

When was she getting married? Her older sister was already married, and she had a younger sister, so she shouldn't wait too long. It wasn't easy to find people as highly educated as she was, and so she shouldn't wait too long. Her body clock was ticking too.

'I was not very happy at the idea at first, but I slowly got used to it,' Sara says. Now that she knew she would have to get married soon, she went about organizing things. She was used to the role—she had headed activity clubs in college, and at work she was essentially paid to tell people how to run their companies.

The first thing she did as she began to look for a partner was to speak to some of her older married friends, and make a list of qualities she would like in a husband. There were two categories:

- ❖ Things which were absolutely necessary
- ❖ Things which she could overlook

Once she had written that down, she knew what she really wanted from marriage. The advice she got from the married couples she spoke to was:

- ❖ You must be happy with yourself
- ❖ You must know what you want before you decide to get married
- ❖ You can't expect that getting married is a solution to all your problems, or will make for a happily-ever-after

Sara approached marriage with the pragmatism she exercised towards most things. She attended a premarital session conducted by a Christian organization, which she says gave her a realistic picture of marriage—what to expect and what not to expect.

'I guess with all the advice and suggestions, and my being clear about what I wanted from a life partner, I knew I was ready for marriage,' she muses.

Armed with her checklist, it would be simpler to figure out whether someone was right for her.

'Of course, I regret that I didn't put "should sing and play the guitar" in the must-have, non-negotiable section,' she laughs. 'I say that every day, and my husband tries to sing, with a lot of effort. But he just might make a decent singer, with training.'

Far from the chai-tray meeting, Sara's first encounter with Sunil Jose had all the trappings of a cinematic love story. She was helping her friend shop, when they ran into Sunil, who happened to be her friend's cousin. They were introduced, and she only said hi, before carrying on with the shopping. They ran into each other once again, with the same friend-cousin, and they got chatting. After this, her friend confessed to her that he had set up the accidental meetings with Sunil, because he thought they might get along, and Sunil's parents were looking out for a girl.

'I kind of liked him because he was very calm, courteous, helpful and thoughtful,' Sara recalls. 'One incident stood out—we saw a very old lady begging, and she looked like she was starving. Rather than giving her money, Sunil went and bought some rice and fruit for the lady. He said that way no one would steal it from her, and she would get her nutrition.'

They finally did have the official meeting with the parents.

'We met in Sunil's parents' place, so it was the reverse. He served us all juice,' Sara says, with a smile. 'That was really going against tradition, and I was very happy about it.'

Is it possible, then, to tailor oneself a perfect match? To make a wish-list, and find a made-to-order partner who fits in perfectly with our ideas of an ideal?

'I don't believe people can expect perfect partners from either a "love" or an "arranged" marriage,' Sara says. 'Whichever it is, you have to be realistic. Many of the older people I spoke to told me this—don't expect that you can change anyone just because you're married to them.'

Pointing out that nowadays even people going in for arranged marriages are given some time to get to know each other, Sara acknowledges that everyone tends to put their best foot forward. Despite this, she believes one still gets to know the things one doesn't like in a partner.

'I knew Sunil was quite absent-minded in the few months I hung out with him, before we got engaged,' she says, 'See, in an arranged marriage, it's true many of the boxes on your or your parents' checklist might get ticked, but it's better not to be idealistic. Somewhere down the line, people change, and situations and circumstances change as well.'

According to her, one of the biggest advantages of an arranged marriage is the fact that one's parents are happy with one's choice of partner.

Setting up home, over and over again

Living in a different country from one's parents isn't easy. And it takes a while to find a routine. But the good thing about the current generation of parents is that they're willing to help.

'Thankfully for me, my mom had come and set up my kitchen in our new place right after we got back from our honeymoon and started work,' Sara confesses. 'It was such a relief! Otherwise I would have been confused and stressed with the whole process. When you live alone, it doesn't matter how your kitchen looks, but once you're married, suddenly everyone expects you to be this wonder woman who knows how to arrange kitchen shelves and all that.'

Her mother helped her set up her home as well. But then they had to move, and Sara missed having her mother around. The process of shifting is arduous, and takes its toll on the woman.

'The wife is expected to do everything—pack, unpack, set up the home,' Sara says, with some frustration. 'If the guy helps, oh, he is *such* a nice husband! In my case, Sunil has tried to help, but that usually becomes double work for me. His sense of aesthetics is quite bad, so he'll set up things without looking into the colour scheme. I end up changing everything, to go with the curtains or whatever. But he's really good when it comes to packing and unpacking electronic gadgets, that much credit I'll give him.'

The real problem came when Sunil had to move to London for a year. At the time, Sara was very happy at work, she had made new friends, and she liked the new flat they had moved into. However, this would be a windfall for Sunil, and great for his career, so she was willing to move. Besides, her sister lived in London, and Sara would get to meet the friends she had gone to university with. The idea of watching the Olympics, and travelling through Europe was enticing.

However, it can be very hard for an intelligent, educated woman to have to give up working, and the restrictions on immigrants made it difficult for her to qualify for a job. Initially, Sara was so busy setting up and getting used to the place that she didn't miss working. Domestic help is expensive, and so she was under some strain, keeping their home tidy. She admits she felt bitter when she began to look for part-time work, because she was constantly aware that she had had to give up a perfectly good job back home. Eventually, she listed the positives:

- ❖ It's a new experience
- ❖ My sister lives in the same city
- ❖ Gluten-free bread is readily available! (Sara had recently been diagnosed with celiac disease)
- ❖ I can always go back to India if I can't take it any more

In sickness and in health

Sara's and Sunil's marriage came with health problems on both sides. Sunil had suffered from repetitive strain injury (RSI), and he had trouble with his hands. He told Sara about this before marriage. Unfortunately, both of them fell ill at the same time. Just as Sunil's hands began to act up, Sara had to deal with stomach upsets, anxiety, falling hair and depression. She thought it was the stress of having to go to work and come back to take care of a house.

'Initially, of course, we were both fighting about it,' she says. 'I would ask him to do things, and he would say he was tired, and I would say I'm tired too. But he was very understanding as well. When I didn't have the energy to cook, he would get something in or ask our part-time help to make something. I felt bad for feeling tired, because I could not do half the things I wanted to do.'

And then, Sara was diagnosed with celiac disease. She wanted to quit her job, and though Sunil didn't want her to at first, he came around when he saw how hard she found balancing both aspects of her life. Even after quitting her job,

Sara took a month to recover. Meanwhile, Sunil's hands took a turn for the worse. He couldn't type, or drive long distances. So she had to take over the driving.

'It was quite a difficult time for us,' she says. 'This is not something most couples face in their first year of marriage—it was a test of our vows, 'in sickness and in health'. But we stuck it out. We did get angry at each other, but we talked, and we prayed together a lot. It's only by God's grace that we saw that period through. It's not easy for people to understand what we went through, but the best part of it was that it made our relationship stronger, and we learned to pick each other up whenever we had to.'

Though Sunil has now recovered from RSI, Sara has her bad days, especially if she has eaten something containing gluten by mistake. Sunil knows what to do if she gets sick, what symptoms he should look out for, and that he should be careful not to use the same cutlery on bread that he does on food meant for Sara. They're quite understanding of each other's need for dependence on the other now, says Sara.

But she does have a grouse with people's attitudes to men and women in a marriage. 'You know, he gets a lot of praise for being understanding. But I never did, for taking care of him when *he* was sick. It's assumed that a woman should take care of her husband in sickness, but a husband's doing the same is attributed to the goodness of his heart or something!' What matters to her, though, is that he appreciates what she does for him.

The silver lining was that Sara didn't have to deal with relatives harassing her to make babies quickly.

In the middle of all this, there's something to be said for marriage, Sara laughs. 'There is always someone you can complain to about your day, or your day at work. If you're sick, you have someone to take you to the doc. You don't have to come back to an empty house. You have a friend who lives with you 24×7. For me, personally, the best thing about being married is that Sunil really understands how sick I can get and what are the dos and don'ts when I'm ill. He reads food labels, looks for gluten-free food wherever he goes, and mostly eats gluten-free food himself so I don't have to cook separately for him. I am not sure even my parents and sisters would do that for me.'

'The foundation of my marriage was tissue paper'

Ruchika Solanki speaks about marrying after heartbreak, creating chemistry in an arranged set-up, and what to do when things don't feel right.

Ruchika Solanki had the sort of love story that everyone wants to tell—she and her boyfriend met at a café in Delhi. She was sitting with her friend, he with his. She and her friend were having an argument over a board game, and she called out to him, because the four of them were the only customers in the café. He took her side, his friend took her friend's, and they all got talking. She and he got together, their friends didn't.

But let's focus on the romance. That day at the café, they exchanged email IDs—students didn't usually have mobile phones, because they were too expensive at the time. And anyway, he was going abroad for higher education. They chatted for a year and a half, as friends, and then he told her he had always liked her. He would be back in Delhi in a few months. For the next three years, they were in a relationship. He was the sober, serious Delhi-bred south Indian, and she was the cheerful, impulsive boarding-school-bred Delhiite.

A year into the relationship, Ruchika knew this was the man she wanted to marry. They met each other's parents. Her parents didn't like him.

'Something about him isn't quite right,' her mother would often say. 'They're not like us.'

Ruchika railed against her conservative mother's reservations, and finally it was all sorted—it was decided they would eventually be married.

However, things went wrong between them. Suddenly they were fighting all the time, and 'issues' kept cropping up. He was taking her for granted, and showed no sign of wanting to get hitched. At home, Ruchika was being pressurized by her family to get married.

After a particularly bad spate of fighting, she broke up with her boyfriend. She took on late shifts at the call centre where she worked, so she could cry in peace. She couldn't cry at home, because she didn't like hearing her mother saying, 'I told you so.'

'And then I realized I should have broken it off much earlier,' she says. 'Maybe my mother knew he wasn't right for me all along. Maybe that's what she meant by "They're not like us." I mean, in our families, men take care of the women. You know, once my new car got stolen. And in Delhi, you can change the number plates, cross over into UP, or Haryana, and that's it. So, I started blubbering on the phone to him, and asked him to come over. He went, "Can't you just get an auto? I'm getting a haircut."' She pauses. 'And you know the worst part? He was bloody bald!'

When it was clear they weren't getting back together, her parents began to look for a groom. Meanwhile, she had found a guy on the rebound, an acquaintance who declared that he had been in love with her for years, and proposed marriage, but she wasn't interested.

'Once I told a friend of mine that I really needed a break from men,' Ruchika recalls. 'And she gave me a look and said, "You know, getting married isn't the ideal route to taking a break from men." But I was fighting all the time with my mother, and both of us would end up crying. I also had this cousin who was held up as a living example of what happened to good girls who didn't get married on time. She had to flee to America, so people would stop asking her questions and talking about her.'

At this point, she didn't care whom she married. She knew she would have to marry. And she knew she wouldn't meet the 'boy' alone until they were engaged. They could meet with the families around once, and they could speak on the phone however often they wanted. Once they were engaged, they could date. She rejected the first few 'boys' outright, because they put her off immediately. And then, she met Rohan.

'I remember sitting in a cabin and waiting for his call,' she says. 'He said he'd call at 9. I didn't want him to call, but I was offended when he was a few minutes late. It was a really messed up state of mind to be in. I just rushed into the whole thing.'

She couldn't think of any reason to marry him, but she couldn't think of any reason not to either. They were duly engaged.

'And then, I thought I would get to know him better. But we went out for coffee once, and then he came home once, and that was it,' she says. 'It had been two months since the engagement, a month and a half left for the wedding, and we'd met twice. They felt like business meetings. We just described what we each did, and spoke about our hometowns. I didn't know him at all, and there was zero chemistry. He hadn't even tried to hold my hand. I couldn't imagine that I would ever sleep with him.'

Everyone told her it was abnormal that he hadn't even held her hand. Even her mother agreed. Ruchika didn't think she could relate to him at all. She was particular about two things—that a man she married should be able to speak his own language properly, and Rohan qualified, because he spoke Hindi and two local dialects; and second, that he should speak the English she spoke. But Rohan spoke 'corporate English'.

'Look, I'd get these messages saying things like, "I'll call you before EoD." I mean, what's that doing in a message to a fiancée?! I know it's an arranged marriage, I'm not asking for bouquets and shayaris and all of that, but please don't put in FYIs and EoDs! And then, he made some grammatical error, and I was like, "Oh God, what have I got myself into?!"'

She wanted to head off to America to holiday by herself, maybe speak to her unmarried and exiled cousin and ask her what she should do. Was life without men really that bad? She decided she would take the bull by the horns and speak to Rohan.

'I was chatting with a friend from work for a long time about this. And I decided I would tell him maybe it wasn't working out between us, and it was best to call it off before the wedding. But, first, I was going to tell him that I felt like holidaying by myself, and see how he reacted.'

Rule 1: When things seem to be wrong, confront them

Ruchika sat down with her friend and they made a mental note of the things she would have to discuss. It was a very long list.

'We needed to write it down, and we didn't have pen or paper,' she laughs. 'So, my friend went and borrowed a pen from an uncle who ran a canteen. He acted like she was asking him for his entire inheritance, but we got the pen. He refused to tear a sheet off his account book though, so we raided the tissue dispenser by the washbasin. And then we made a list of the things I'd speak about.'

It read something like this:

* Holidaying abroad—also, honeymoon, because he's not mentioned it . . . why?
* No chemistry—not even holding hands
* Expectations? Why does he want to marry? Then, why marry you?
* Can't relate to him
* Is he being forced into this? Why only two meetings since engagement?
* Call off?

There were more points, but she doesn't remember them now. She sent him a text: 'Need to talk to you. Please call when free.'

Rohan sensed the urgency, and called immediately. She took the call outside the canteen, with her friend sitting beside her, and making more points on tissue paper, as she listened in on half the conversation.

'The poor man got a shock when I told him I wanted to go off on holiday. He said, "Let's wait till the wedding, and we can both go,"' she laughs. 'And then he told me he'd been worried that I would think he was too forward, and that's why he hadn't even held my hand.'

She didn't go abroad by herself. They went to America on their honeymoon.

'And he kissed me the next time we went out,' she giggles. 'I went to office and told my friends the next day, and those crazy girls gave me a standing ovation. This middle-aged colleague of ours asked what was going on, and they told him it was my birthday. Poor thing, he went and bought me a pastry. It was super-embarrassing.'

After marriage

As long as you stay practical, Ruchika feels a marriage can work. You need to get the basics right, whether it's about holding hands and honeymooning, or about sorting out finances, or about what matters to you, or about when you want to have children, or about whether you want to continue to work.

'I keep teasing him about his "corporate English",' she says with a smile, 'and he joins in, writing "IMHO" and things like that in texts to me on purpose. Now, I find it funny.'

She also says there has been no problem with the chemistry, and she can't remember why it was so difficult for them to hold hands. When he's away on business trips, she 'misses him like crazy'.

'And I keep thinking—the foundation of my marriage was a piece of tissue paper.'

'You can't hide and seek'

Smriti Rao tells us why one needs to be ready to put oneself out there, if one intends to find a life partner.

At 28, Smriti Rao was doing very well in her career. A branding and talent development consultant, she had lived in four metros over the past few years, and worked in fields that ranged from education to brand management to corporate training. Her professional life was on a high, but she was beginning to feel the need for companionship.

'I think there's a stage in your twenties when you're at your narcissistic best,' Smriti says, with a laugh. 'It probably happens at different times for different people. You want companionship, but you basically want you—someone who is exactly like you, but a male version. I think it happens mostly to people who get external recognition from family and work. You're told you're bright, you're funny, you're creative, you're *different*, and it spills into this whole self-image where you begin to feel, "Will I find someone who is good enough for me?"'

Looking back, Smriti says she was very certain about what she wanted, and what life she saw for herself when she was 19–20 years old. Through her twenties, her goals blurred out. 'The nice part is that everyone puts a positive spin on it, and says how adventurous I am, and how exposed to different cities and cultures. But the truth is that I was just wandering, unclear, and I think just trying to find my feet in something professionally, and also trying to figure out what I wanted from a relationship. I think I gradually started piecing that in together only when I was nearing 30, when I decided to actually settle down.'

But even though she agreed to meet people, her heart was not in it. She giggles that the profile that was circulated in the 'matchmaking circle' was practically a CV. It said nothing about what kind of person she was looking for, or what she wanted to do with her life. 'Not even my hobbies were mentioned. But, I would check out other profiles, and nitpick. I mean, who the hell lists their hobbies as "singing" and "dancing"?'

Smriti feels a certain kind of woman tends to dread the idea of arranged marriage. 'Maybe it goes with the breadth of exposure in terms of the places we live in and the jobs we do. Or, maybe it goes back to the narcissism I spoke about. I got into the whole thing with a very detached attitude, without any expectations.'

One of the biggest challenges she spotted was dealing with the unrealistic expectations and the disproportionate importance our society accords to *appearance*. 'I'm sure all women get advice about how you should lose weight, not get tanned in the sun, and that you should do a facial before meeting the guy and so on, and there are women who can let that pass and say "Okay, I'll do all that so that I can look my best that day." But people who already have very low self-esteem, or a poor body image of themselves, are likely to take that as a comment on their inadequacy, and that's what happened to me.'

She realized that one's choice of partner depends on how one sees oneself at the time. This became the trigger for an unreal weight-loss regime. 'My weight was just the most convenient thing to control, whether I'm fat or thin, and how that made me feel, with respect to how adequate I am.'

Around this time, Smriti started thinking about the other marriages in her family. Though none of her cousins had had arranged marriages, they had all married within the Konkani community; many had found partners in the family-friend circle. She had never seen herself marrying in the community—her friends' circle was mixed.

'I think my upbringing was in a very simple, close-knit, Konkani setting,' she says. 'It's not as urbane and diverse as I used to think it was; if you look inside at the basics of who you are, you realize there's a comforting sense of familiarity. I think that's where the readiness to go into an arranged marriage came from.'

When she went to meet Sagar, she hadn't even checked out his profile or picture. But she could see that he was focused, that he had got into the arranged marriage circuit with the intention of finding a bride.

'I did have some idea that he was right for me, but I didn't know why I felt that way. I didn't have a checklist of criteria,' she grins. 'I just knew something fit. I took a blind plunge, and I think I realized what I wanted only once I got married. The kind of person that I am, I tend to go by instinct—whether it comes to choosing a job, or friends, or how I communicate, or whom I trust. I've a good, deep, solid instinct on a lot of things.'

Buoyed by her sense that things could work out, Smriti agreed to marry Sagar within a month. She says a lot of things fell in place for her after marriage. 'Or, maybe my belief in the institution was why it fell into place,' she laughs.

Turning serious, she says she doesn't think one can make a cerebral decision about marriage. People may ask you to weigh your options, and set your criteria, but often the flow of your life guides you towards a particular decision.

'You can set a standard on anything—funniness, or brightness, or language, or how well-informed someone is—but it doesn't make sense if you're not sure of what you want,' Smriti says. She feels it is only in retrospect that she can see what she was really looking for, and that her initial approach may not have been right.

'I had lost faith in my ability to pick the right kind of people, and the problem was that I wasn't clear about what I wanted. We don't realize that people can be articulate in different ways, and creative in different ways, and funny in different ways. This search for someone who is exactly like you satisfies a very transient need. I was very, very worried about not finding someone who will understand the things I said, the way I said them. As it is, even among my friends, there's just a handful who do. But I think that sort of thinking is highly overrated by us, since it's clearly not catering to more fundamental, significant parts of us.'

The significant part, she would later find, pointed to a deeper yearning, for respect, affection, acceptance and stability. The fact that someone who caters to one's idea of a perfect partner often fails to satisfy these needs can lead to a disconnect that is frustrating.

'At some point, you see that all your relationships are reflections of your sense of self, and then you don't know what you want in a man.'

Under such circumstances, how do you go about your search for a partner who fits in with what you need?

'You can't hide and seek. The problem is there are lots of us who don't want to put ourselves out there, but still want to find a life partner,' Smriti says. 'You need to be willing to take a chance. You can't project something else, or be someone else in order to be more acceptable in the marriage mandi. You have to brace yourself, and go out there, meet people, maybe be a bit vulnerable.'

Of course, one of the big worries is that one may end up saying too much, revealing too much about oneself to a stranger, with whom there may never be a connection. Smriti says one's willingness to put oneself out there often depends on one's acceptance of oneself. There is a lot that we ourselves reject about our lives, especially the things we did in our twenties.

The challenge is to find someone who's open and mature enough to grant you the acceptance that you may not grant yourself about yourself, she says. 'One of my scariest experiences was introducing Sagar to old friends,' Smriti recalls. 'I didn't plan a meet-the-fiancé sort of event, though he actually arranged for me to meet *his* friends. But a couple of months before our wedding, I decided to introduce him to my friends from Mumbai, where I went to college. And I was a real brat back then. I'd be running about in shorts and playing basketball, and that's who they know me as. I realized how much I'd changed since then only when my colony friends went on about how I've become so quiet and so inhibited and so different, and what's with all the gracefulness! And then, you start wondering about whether you're faking this. It feels like two islands meeting—the early-twenties'-Smriti and grown-up Smriti—and I was very confused. Suddenly, there was this big fear that Sagar would reject who I used to be.'

The first year of marriage will be filled with more such fears and doubts, Smriti says, and how you deal with them sets the tone for the marriage. Whatever your instinct says about a person, and how much ever information you gather about him, marriage is a new ball game.

'The thing you come in most unprepared for is the realness of it—the decisions you need to make, the kind of different aspirations you both may have, sharing what makes you happy and exposing what makes you sad, who demonstrates affection, who takes charge, etcetera . . . this *realness* of making it work.'

This realness can manifest in ways we shudder to think about before tying the knot. 'Marriage involves seeing each other at their ugliest worst. Like sitting with a red, snotty face, or bawling about the stupidest thing. Then you wake up the next day, still feeling attracted to that person. Everyone talks about compatibility, about measuring how suited you are to each other a little ahead, but I think you can only know compatibility if you truly know what you want. And you figure out only when you have it whether you want it or not. It's a big chance to take.'

The important thing is to give oneself enough time to understand the other person, and vice versa, Smriti says. One will continually find out things about one's partner and about oneself, and somewhere, a couple finds harmony. And when that happens, the plunge is so worth it!

A friend of mine told me about a cousin of hers who had been registered on matrimonial websites as well as marriage bureaus. Her profile was a three-page résumé, with emphasis on her culinary skills and her knowledge of handicrafts. The response was disappointing, and expressions of interest came in mainly from families that the girl couldn't see herself marrying into.

When her B-school graduate brother came down on holiday, he had a look at the profile, and decided it needed to be shaken up. 'It underplays her talents, and we need to showcase her better,' he said.

He set to it with the same approach he would use on a company profile. He put down the languages she knew, emphasized that she had grown up in various environments—southern India, north India and abroad—and that she was 'easy to get along with', had 'good interpersonal skills', that she was willing to travel, and open to new cultures, and therefore all right with settling abroad. He wrote that she had done a diploma in fashion design, which showed the world she was traditional enough to pose in a Kanchivaram sari, but hip enough to dress models up. Finally, he revamped the pictures they had uploaded, and the responses began to flood in.

Dealing with changing priorities

Madhumitha Prasad speaks of how people and priorities change after marriage, and tells us how a woman shouldn't lose sight of either her career or her family.

Madhumitha Prasad got married when she was 24 years old. In the eight years since then, she has had a child, moved cities thrice, moved countries once, and gone back to work. She feels an early marriage makes sense. And 24 didn't strike her as particularly early, because most of her friends were also getting married around the time.

She's candid about the advantages of getting married when she was in her early twenties. 'I guess the pool of guys you can choose from is more when you are young. This pool shrinks as you age, and you may end up with rejects.'

The real challenge, she says, is dealing with changing priorities after marriage. 'Marriage is a gamble,' she says. Half the outcome depends on the cards you pick, and the rest on how you play those cards.

'What I mean is, fifty per cent of the work is done before the marriage—when you try to get to know your spouse, when you talk to each other, do your background checks on the person and the family. And this holds good whether it is a love match or an arranged marriage. The rest depends on the effort the couple makes for the marriage to work. Sacrifices, adjustments and patching up after a fight should come from both sides. That said, if you've picked the wrong person, no amount of sacrifice or adjustment will help.'

Knowing someone is right

Madhumitha had dated people before she decided to have an arranged marriage. 'I'd made a few wrong decisions earlier, and sort of gave up on finding the right guy. So I bestowed the responsibility on my family,' she says. 'Frankly I was not really attracted to Prasad before marriage. The only reason I said yes to him, honestly, was that there was no reason to say no. I entered matrimony with doubts on whether I had made the right decision. Thankfully I had.'

She doesn't trust instinct, and doesn't believe one can simply 'know' when someone is right. 'I think a little compatibility check should be done.' In her case, it so happened that a friend had worked with Prasad earlier. 'She told me that he was a nice, decent guy and that sort of gave me the confidence. And, of course, we met and talked to each other, and I felt we would get along.'

The first year of marriage left her worried though. 'We both fought like mad, making me wonder many times whether I had made a huge mistake. But then I also knew that he was a nice guy at heart. I guess he would have thought the same about me. Both of us made that little effort to patch up, to work on the marriage, and here we are now.'

Changing priorities

Say what you will about modern women and an advanced society, but Madhumitha feels priorities change more for women after marriage, at least in the Indian family structure. 'Here, marriage means moving into a new household, both literally *and* in terms of our identity as a member of another family. You need to make the in-laws feel important. I don't mean to sound docile, but making the in-laws feel respected will ensure that the family boat doesn't rock—unhappy in-laws would also mean an unhappy husband. That does not mean giving up your career, likes or needs. But open communication really helps here. Once your people know how good you are, or your intentions are, you don't even have to make a conscious effort to make them feel wanted or comfortable.'

The other tricky aspect of marriage for a working woman is the challenge of balancing her home and her career. In Madhumitha's case, she shifted cities with her husband several times. The biggest problem she has had to confront is career growth. She works in the finance sector, and he in IT.

'Again, it depends on priorities,' she says. 'I was working in Mumbai, and just a year after marriage, he got a job in Hyderabad. Half-heartedly, I moved out of Mumbai. I told him, "This time, I've sacrificed my career for you. Next time, you should do it for me." I could have stayed on in Mumbai, while he went to Hyderabad. But I really do not believe in long-distance relationships, and we were just getting to know each other at the time. Now, having been married for eight years, we have decided that even if Prasad has to move out to a new city to follow his career, I will stay where I am, if that will help my career.'

When he had to move to the US, she made sure the visa regulations would allow her to start working soon. The work permit came through within a few months of their move, and her job search is on, but she decided to keep herself occupied in the interim. She started learning Spanish and conducting music classes for children, to keep herself busy. 'And I still tell him that once again I have sacrificed my job for him, to ensure that he does not forget it and adjusts for me the next time.'

But she acknowledges that one can't have it all. 'No woman I know does. Either they have a great career, or a great personal life. You may have both, but no children. Or, you have problem kids. Or, you have wonderful children, but you've got health issues. God is very fair. He distributes the spoils and troubles evenly.'

The mechanics of a modern marriage

Can we take it for granted that our generation of men will help around the house, and share chores and babysitting duties? Or is the onus still on women to keep the house running? Madhumitha weighs her answer. 'A good part of the onus *is* on women. But how you train your hubby is also a factor. A few women I know have trained their husbands beautifully into sharing household work. I would say it is also better to talk about these things with the guy before you enter matrimony. That way neither of you is heading for a shock. A friend of mine thought her fiancé was kidding when he said he would not help around in the house. He really did not, after marriage, and she felt like a fool.'

In parting, she has a bit of advice for newly married people: 'Put in a sincere effort to make the marriage work. If it still doesn't, don't waste the rest of your life with him or her. There are women like Jaya Bachchan and Hillary Clinton who stay in marriages for their own reasons. I like such women too. But if you're not getting anything like that out of it, walk out.'

Is marrying young a mistake?

Vaidehi Raman tells us why getting married when one is too young to know one's own mind can be disastrous

Vaidehi Raman, 38, is among the proponents of a reasonably late marriage. She dismisses the notion that getting married early allows one to grow with the person one marries. 'You grow *out* of it very quickly,' she says, wryly. A technical writer and quality controller by profession, Vaidehi married when she was just 21, right out of college, and before she had taken up a job. Her husband was seven years older.

Marriage threw her into a world that was entirely different from the one she had grown up in. Her father was in government service, and so she grew up mostly in the North. When they moved to Madras, she spoke very little Tamil, and was far more comfortable with English and Hindi. Marrying a man who didn't speak Hindi was something she *could* deal with, but she was to find out the milieu she was marrying into was drastically different from the one she was raised in.

'I grew up wearing jeans and skirts, but there were all these ground rules when I got married. He forbade my wearing chikankari salwars. I used to love them, and I would always wear them with a slip, but he wouldn't allow it. Jeans were not allowed. And there were these other instructions—don't stand outside the house, don't talk to my friends . . . the thing is, you won't take any of it when you're older, but at 21, I was very innocent. I would think, "Oh, my husband should be happy, I should do what he likes, I should be what he wants me to be." It's only later that you realise there's nothing wrong with wanting happiness for yourself."

She hadn't spent much time with her to-be husband—she was married to him within two months of the first meeting—and so she had no idea what sort of person he was. 'We didn't spend time together at all. He never took me out. His reasoning was that, if people saw us together, and then the marriage was called off for some reason, no one else would marry me. If someone says that when you're a bit older, you would sense the paranoia and conservativeness. But as a 21-year-old, you don't realize that it makes no sense. It all hits you in retrospect.'

While Vaidehi hesitates to make a blanket statement, and acknowledges that everything depends on the kind of person one marries, and whether one is able to adapt to a new situation, she believes maturity is a crucial factor in knowing how to handle a relationship.

'It also depends on the way you've been brought up. If you've seen a lot of conflict in your family, you know it happens, and that it gets resolved. If you're coming in from a cocoon, and you're suddenly exposed to a conflict situation, you don't know what to do, and then the trouble starts. In my case, it had been just the three of us—me and my parents—all my life, and we never had big disagreements. Everything was just. Of course, we had small fights, but no one ill-treated anybody.'

The rules she had to follow in her husband's home were bad enough, but Vaidehi began to feel the lack of support intensely when she became pregnant, soon after marriage. 'My mother-in-law used to make one big vessel of *kara kuzhambu* (a type of spicy sambar) in the morning, and some oily vegetable, and I would have only that to eat till night. I wasn't allowed to cook. My husband's salary went directly to his mother, and I wasn't earning, so I had no access to money, and I couldn't buy food from outside. What do you do when you're not able to handle something when you're pregnant, or when you find it too repulsive to eat? Are you supposed to starve the whole day?'

Her husband didn't come to her defence; he expected her to toe his mother's line. She had no one to turn to, except her parents, and they would ask her to adjust. 'They would tell me you have to pull on, things will be fine. At that age, you can't discuss these things with your friends. You feel so ashamed, and so disgusted that you're in that kind of situation and that you can't do anything about it.'

Often, she would find herself sitting alone, in tears. Things got worse when she had to handle a baby, on top of a complicated relationship, at 22. Her husband would go out with his friends on weekends, while Vaidehi was left alone with the baby, and her mother-in-law, who didn't help much with the child.

'Every time I asked him to take me out, he would say it

was too expensive, and that I didn't know the value of money because I wasn't earning. It used to hurt me very much back then, but then you slowly get hardened to these things. Time has a way of moulding you. The more and more you're exposed to hardship, the fewer things pierce through your armour. It's the tougher things that hurt you. After a few more years, even those won't hurt you. And then, finally, you start giving in to your situation. It can turn into Stockholm Syndrome almost.'

Vaidehi speaks of cases in the newspapers, where women are ill-treated by their in-laws, especially when something untoward—such as a death—occurs soon after the wedding, and that is associated with the ill luck a bride brings.

'That's another problem in our society. People illogically blame the woman for everything,' Vaidehi says. 'Even in my case, my husband didn't get along with many of his relatives; but the neighbours used to think they didn't come home because I wasn't warm enough. These things are especially hard to endure when you're too young to know the world.'

Of course, there are women who go through emotional and physical abuse, who are not even allowed to stay in touch with their parents and siblings. There are those who are so traumatized they commit suicide, or who succumb with docility to everything they must endure, and blame it all on fate. Most fall into severe depression. And such marriages are not restricted to uneducated women, or women from low-income families.

Knowing what a bad marriage could do, Vaidehi was tempted to walk out of her own. Every time she brought it up with her parents, they would talk her out of it. Eventually, they came to live with Vaidehi, so that they could help her out. That came about by chance.

Raman had always wanted to marry a working woman, but once he met Vaidehi, he changed his mind. However, he began to insist that she go to work, after marriage. She did take up a job, but found that her toddler wasn't being looked after well enough by her mother-in-law. 'Thankfully, my sister-in-law wanted her to come live with her, and so she moved out. When Raman wanted me to continue working, I insisted that I needed my parents to move in with us. So, he had no choice. Luckily for me, my parents agreed. They sold their flat, gave me the money to use as down payment for a bigger flat, and moved in.'

Vaidehi says it isn't easy managing a home that houses both one's parents and husband. 'Your husband will start complaining that your mother watches TV at home, your mother will start complaining that your husband doesn't give the servant space to clean up properly, and everyone gives the maid a separate set of instructions. But, fortunately, rapport or no rapport, my parents have stayed on with me.'

Initially, her husband threatened to walk out of the house every time there was a dispute. Vaidehi's friends told her it wasn't a good idea to live with her parents. But she remained firm. 'I'm very clear about this—they will stay with us. For one thing, they're getting old and I'm their only child. For another, they are *my* support system, and they've kept me sane. And for a third, they sold their house so I could buy one . . . do you really expect me to ask them to move to rented accommodation?'

Her advice to women who are looking to get married is:

❖ First, get to know your prospective husband, make sure he's someone you can get along with, you're compatible with

❖ Lay down the rules, and see that you're not simply taking over chores from his mother or maid or both—that is compromise with no hope of reprieve

❖ If you know it's not working, walk out before it's too late

❖ If you can't walk out, turn to your parents, and keep them with you

'Honestly, my parents are the reason I'm standing here, alive, with my child here today,' she says, 'And though there were times when I felt entrapped, I somehow mustered the courage not to yield to him. Say what you will, do what you will, if you want to leave me, you can; but they will stay.'

The parents' role

Though Vaidehi says her parents have been there for her, she isn't able to get over her resentment against them for getting her married to Raman.

'Even though my parents are helping me now, every time there is a disagreement, or unpleasantness, the first thing I do is blame them. And this is the first sentence out of my mouth—either you should have waited till I had got a job and was older, or you should have done a thorough background check to find out what he's all about, or given me some time to understand things about him, or you should have let me leave him when I wanted to. It's a life you're playing with. It's not like you chose a wrong subject, and can quit your course and choose the right one next year. It's sad when a marriage doesn't work the way it should.'

One of the biggest problems with the arranged marriage system is that a lot of parents feel getting their daughters married off is a duty they need to tick off a list, Vaidehi says, whereas the first thing they need to realize is that the issue is making sure their daughters are happy, not that their daughters are married.

In many cases, they may not even be willing to help the daughter out, or claim any ownership of or responsibility for her after marriage. There are those parents who would be too concerned about the freedoms they would have to give up—living in their own space, watching what they want on television, and having to accommodate the preferences of their daughters' in-laws—to consider moving in with their daughters.

Vaidehi admits she is lucky that her parents did not hesitate to give up all of that. But she wishes they had supported her when she first said she wanted to walk out of her marriage, a year into it. 'If only they had said then that I could get a job, they would help me with the baby, I would be better off, I feel. At 22, you don't have the guts to walk out into the street, alone with a baby. At least, I didn't.'

However, perhaps because he was raised by her parents, her son has become part of her support system too. 'Now, my husband has toned down because my son puts his foot down, and argues with him, and talks back to him in a way that I couldn't.'

Knowing when to leave

While Vaidehi's marriage has got better with time, it isn't the life she would have chosen had she been a few years older, she says. 'Of course, even then, if I'd not been employed, I might have had trouble. Because the moment you start earning, it makes a big difference. You know you can manage on your own, you know you actually don't need a man. What do you need a man for?'

And the most dangerous thing with being submissive in a marriage is that it can spill over to the rest of one's life, especially when one is young.

'Even at work, that used to happen to me. I would be a pushover. I used to be shocked at how people could behave so badly, how they could treat other people like that. But then I realised that's how you should be, if you want people not to walk all over you. It's changed my perspective completely. And now, I give it right back to him when he tries to put me down. It gives me the satisfaction that at least I'm not a dumb witness to what is going on here.'

But she warns that this could take a toll on children. 'When you're fighting all the time, your kid won't have much respect for either of you, nor will he feel secure and happy. And however determined you are, you *will* end up having arguments in front of your kids.'

Vaidehi feels it's a bad idea to stay on in a marriage for the children. It isn't healthy for them to be exposed to an ugly environment. 'And I've been lucky in that my child stands

101

up for me. The thing is, mothers tend to keep their children away from knowing about the turbulence in a marriage—we imagine they won't sense it. Whereas, some men poison their children against their wives. There are a lot of women I know whose children despise them, and prefer the father. On the other hand, even if this is not the case, once the children get used to a particular kind of lifestyle, the kind that a double income will provide, it becomes too hard to leave.'

Yet, she says there are some things no woman should take— such as physical abuse, sexual abuse, or infidelity—even if she has children. 'You must walk out of something like that, because even if they don't understand now, they will understand why you had to do it later, when they're older. If something like that had happened, I *would* have left.'

It's not that hard to figure out whether a marriage can work. 'There are small things, insignificant things that men do for their wives. It could be as simple as making soup or hot rasam when you have fever. Those are the little things that show you they love and respect you. Respect has to come from love, it can't come without. So either you must be ready to say I don't need love, from Day One. I don't know if it would be a meaningful relationship, a true one. Anyway, the other option is realizing there's no point living a farce, and walking out early enough.'

Mark your territory

Shwetha Srinivasan tells us how an early marriage worked out for her, how she showed her in-laws their young bride was no pushover, and how she handled an MBA at IIM while running a home and having a baby.

Shwetha Srinivasan knew that she would be married off before she turned 23. Early marriages are the norm in her family, and she had broken a barrier by waiting until she hit her twenties. However, she wasn't going to let marriage and children get in the way of her studies or career. She knew she would have to be clever about planning her life. She would eventually have a lucrative run in the IT industry, do her MBA from the Indian Institute of Management, Bangalore, and segue into brand management for a well-known company—*and* have a child before she turned 30. This is the story of how she did it all.

'I have one cousin, who's six to seven years older, and she was married off in her third year of B.Com.,' she laughs, 'so, I pre-negotiated terms with my parents. When I was in the twelfth, I told them I would mess up my board exams unless they promised to let me finish my degree in peace. In college, I gave them that choice again. Finally, they said they would give me two years after my Bachelor's degree, in which time I could work, do my MS, stay at home, whatever. But they would start looking in the second year, and would get me married by the end of that year. When I turned 22, my entire family was in a panic about me.'

Shwetha was not allowed to date—'my mother would have thrown me off the balcony'—and, anyway, she says she couldn't seriously see herself with anyone. 'When you're 21−22, the guys who are into you are 23−24. Their idea of love is *DDLJ*. They'll watch that, and come give you a bouquet. And seeing that bouquet would give my mother palpitations.'

As her time began to run out, Shwetha gave her family 'a lot of KPIs [Key Performance Indicators]' that her prospective husband should satisfy.

'My first condition was that he should be from my school. My family persuaded me to consider people from an equally reputed one. Then, my second was that he must have done his engineering degree from a good college—no Dindugal College of Engineering types; it had to be Anna University. And he should have at least one degree higher than I did. I was already a B.Tech. And I knew a guy with all this would most likely be in the US, so I gave them one more condition—I would not marry anyone who was outside India.'

Her parents managed to find a groom with a PhD, who lived in Bangalore. She made a final attempt at putting off marriage, saying she wouldn't marry anyone who was more than four years older than she was—the groom her parents had found was seven years older.

'And then, they said no one could have studied as much as I wanted them to study by the time they were 25−26, so I would have to wait a few years if I wanted to limit the age gap to four years. By that time, boys like this would be snapped up. I couldn't argue with that logic. So, I made two big compromises—school and age.'

The two of them spoke to each other over a month, getting to know each other. 'That itself was apparently too long, by our parents' standards. My mother said that within a week they knew from the way we were talking to each other that this would work out. There had been only one guy before him, and I *really* didn't like that one at all. So anyway, at the end of the month, we thought we were calling the shots and announced that we were okay with marriage. But the parents went, "Oh, yeah, we knew. The engagement is on such-and-such day, the wedding is at such-and-such venue", and we were like, *hello*?!'

How does one figure out whether someone is right for one? 'You *don't* know!' Shwetha says simply, 'I could give you some gyan like, "Ohhhh, you look into his eyes and you just *know*", but fact is, you don't. You go in blind. Especially at that age, at 22–23, unless a man is psycho and brands you with cigarette butts, you won't be able to even make the decision to walk out. It's a risk, a big one. You have no clue, you don't know anything about him, all you know is it's a leap of faith. You do the math. If the family backgrounds are similar and you're from the same caste, you assume you won't have problems with cuisine. Then you check horoscopes, and do your permutations and combinations of what is right and what is wrong, and you have it in black and white. So, that filters out some of the risk.'

Though it isn't particularly modern to believe in horoscopes, Shwetha feels they give one a sense of clarity. But she was firm that she did not want horoscopes coming in after she had met someone. 'I told them to do their homework, examine his hair, check his teeth, do whatever, and then put me in touch after they were satisfied with everything. Don't check horoscopes and say it doesn't work after telling me this awesome guy exists, or making me meet him. I don't want that sort of mess. I don't know how many matches passed me by because of the horoscope thing, but I didn't feel the frustration of knowing this was standing in the way of a good match because my parents didn't tell me about any prospect unless the horoscopes were compatible. Thing is, everyone is scared of what people will say if something goes wrong after marriage. The first thing people want to know is, "Didn't you check horoscopes?" And it's mostly out of fear of that, that people check, I think.'

However, all the math and checklists in the world can't prepare a woman for marriage, Shwetha says. One assumes a similar background means a similar home, but the way the in-laws run a home may be very different from the way one's parents do.

'There will be a lot of problems in the beginning—a lot more protocol, a lot more permissions,' she says, 'Marriage brings some amount of liberty, in the sense that you're considered grown-up enough to make your own decisions. But now and then, something crops up, for which you're expected to consult everyone. Little things come as a shocker.'

In Shwetha's case, her in-laws had far more conservative views than her parents. Her mother-in-law sat her down and told her they observed a certain code of conduct when women were menstruating. 'It was considered unclean in their house. At my place, it was no big deal. It was a private thing. You wouldn't go to temples, but you don't announce to everyone that it's because you have your period. I was completely bewildered when my mother-in-law told me this, because my trip was—why should everyone know?'

Dealing with the in-laws: pick your battles

Shwetha didn't have to live with her in-laws, since she and her husband were based in Bangalore, and the in-laws in Chennai. But she did have to stay with them on certain occasions, like Pongal and Deepavali.

'My idea of waking up early is 5.30 in the morning,' she says. 'But the entire household would be up at 4 a.m. That's a little too much, no? The worst part is no one will tell you these things. They expect you to sense it. It's not like they'll come and shake you awake or splash a bucket of water on you. They will be up and about, and you know you can't sleep in, because then it'll be like, "Ooooh, the daughter-in-law is *still* asleep!" If they tell you what to do, you can follow it. But there's this austere, disapproving, deafening silence.'

The toughest part of the deal was coordinating her siesta timings. Her in-laws would wake up at 4 a.m. and then sleep from 11 a.m. to 3 p.m. Shwetha's day would begin at 11 a.m.

irrespective of when she woke up, and she would feel sleepy by 3 p.m.

'Just when I'm about to doze off, they'll wake up and gasp because there's no coffee in the house. Aaaaaaargh!' she shudders.

But being a young bride doesn't mean one has to be a timid bride, and Shwetha says it is important to lay down one's terms. She had to travel frequently between Bangalore and Chennai on work, and her in-laws expected her to stay with them and not with her parents. 'When my husband is around, I can understand that I must stay with my in-laws. But even when he's not there, they'd want me to stay with them because I was supposedly their property now, and that's the protocol. I said, well, balls to you.'

She told them she would visit them, but would stay with her parents. 'If I'm in Chennai for five days, then maybe I'd spend one night at their place. That became a big fight. You ask your parents, they'll tell you that you have to adjust. And your husband will have no clue how to tackle this. He can't go against his parents and say, "Let my wife do what she wants", because then they'll be like, "Ohhhhh, she's got him wrapped around her little finger!"'

Shwetha's husband told her to deal with it however she saw fit, and opted to stay out of the controversy. Her in-laws resented her insistence on staying with her parents in the beginning, but over time things settled down.

'The thing is that you can't take crap from your in-laws. Even now, eight years after I got married, they say stuff like, "It isn't proper for your parents to visit you so often." I immediately retorted with, "What do you mean, it's not proper? They come here to help me with the baby. You didn't offer to, so why do you have a problem with my parents stepping in?" The moment you say that out loud, you become the bad guy. But then they'll know you'll give it right back to them, and they won't mess with you. For all this to happen, it's important to have your husband's support. If he says, "How dare you speak to my parents like that?", of course things will get ugly. It's with these small things that your husband will really help you. Sometimes, he says do what you want. Sometimes, he'll say, "Why do you want to bother getting into a fight now? Just compromise this once, no?" So that's how you figure out whether he's right for you.'

Shwetha also found a support system in her husband's brother's wife, who has it easier, since she lives abroad. 'She comes in for ten days every year or every two years, and she won't bring jeans along. She has an 'India wardrobe', with some ten saris and salwars. And when she's here, there will be some wedding in the family, and she'll put on her nine-yard sari, and be the picture-perfect daughter-in-law. Once, my parents-in-law asked me to take a cue from her. I told them outright, "I can play the dutiful daughter-in-law for ten days a year too; I can't put on an act all year round." They were shocked. But then, they went and stayed with her for some six months, and finally figured out they had two terrible daughters-in-law.'

With a laugh, Shwetha says she and her sister-in-law are really good friends. 'Once she does that weekly Skype chat with them, she calls me up, and laughs for some five minutes non-stop. She tells me everything they're going to crib about, and we get it all out of our system. So, when I speak to them, I can be all silent and downcast, without getting into hysterics.'

It also helps that her parents-in-law are too inexpressive for tiffs to turn into shouting matches. 'When they're elated, you'll see a halfway smile on their faces. When they're pissed, they turn quiet. With my father-in-law, well, if you want to understand how he operates, I can draw a parallel to the programming world. He's like a simple "C" program. He initializes himself at the start of every year, allocates around 400 words in his memory space. So, it's 'ptr = malloc (400)'. That's all he speaks, and it's distributed evenly among children, daughters-in-law and everyone else. From that, you take off Happy New Year, Happy Birthday, Happy Anniversary, Happy Deepavali, Happy Pongal and all of that, and then you have 200 left. That's spent on hi, hello, how are you, come in and so on. After that, even if he wants to speak more, he can't, because the word limit is exhausted. It's what happens when you move the pointer beyond the allocated memory—the "C" program tries to dereference a null pointer, and core dumps. So he will core dump if he talks more. Instead, he sends me all these emails, stating which areas I've disappointed him in, and where I must improve. I find it hilarious. He has his own list of KPIs, and he puts down details of why he has the perception that I don't love them enough and so on. Now, my theory of 400 words holds good, so he can't talk to me, he only writes. It's just too funny!'

However, the hardest part of a marriage is not so much dealing with in-laws as putting food on the table, Shwetha says.

Irrespective of whether one has a cook or not, it's the wife who has to plan for it, buy the groceries and confront the realities of running a house.

'For me, it was especially difficult, because I had never been away from home, either while studying or while working, for two years before marriage. And things were crazy after marriage because I was constantly travelling. So for some two years, we continued to live in his bachelor pad. You know how that is—he thought a doormat needn't really be a doormat, it could be an old banian!'

Studying after marriage

Shwetha had always wanted to do an MBA, right from when she was in college. Her husband had had the luxury of time to finish studying before marriage, whereas she hadn't.

'See, I was adamant—read, foolish—enough to say, if I don't do an MBA from IIM, I would not do one at all. Waiting till after marriage was not a choice. My courtship with CAT was long enough to make a *The Bold and the Beautiful* season . . . don't judge me, I didn't really watch those. But seriously, that ambition to do an MBA was always there, and didn't go away when I got married.'

Though she had to devote a chunk of her time to running the house, and share the rest between herself and her spouse, Shwetha's desire to get her IIM-branded MBA stayed strong. She says her husband encouraged her to go ahead. 'Well, actually, it was the reverse psychology that totally worked. I got in.'

She was juggling work and a part-time MBA. At this time, she decided she could throw a baby into the mix. She was getting older, and she wanted to have a baby before she hit the '30 barrier'. Shwetha explains, 'When you go to a gynaecologist, the first thing she'll ask you is how old you are. At 25, you just have to do the basic blood tests. Once you cross 26, they ask you to do a gestational diabetic test, and so on. Once you're 30, there's trouble—you have to do a lot more.'

All around her, colleagues and classmates who were in the 28–29 age group were rushing to have their first children before they turned 30. Seeing them all have babies, take three months off and come back, reassured Shwetha that she could do it too.

'It worked well for me, but again, it was a big risk. Thankfully, you're allowed to take a break for a quarter or two, while doing a part-time MBA. Also, doing all this can get stressful, and you need to be careful about your health when you're pregnant. So, I gave up my job, and just saw to the MBA and having the baby.'

With time on her hands, she found that she could study a lot better. Once she had the baby, she needed help to finish her MBA. Her mother used to travel to Bangalore from Chennai every alternate week, so that Shwetha could go to classes on Fridays and Saturdays. The other two weeks, her husband would work out of home on Fridays. 'My baby was only four months old. Without that sort of support, I couldn't have completed my MBA.'

Even so, it wasn't easy. She would study while rocking her baby to sleep. During class, she would find herself rocking back and forth, from force of habit. But she chose to do all of that,

Shwetha says, and she had to deal with it. When asked what women who plan to study after getting married and having a baby, should keep in mind, she's quick to list out pointers:

(a) Don't waste time!

'For you to be sitting in class and listening to a lecture, some five people are working in the background. Make the most of it,' Shwetha says.

The constant guilt that she shouldn't be wasting time made her more efficient. Compared to her school and college days, she worked much harder, faster and with more concentration. She even topped some of the subjects. 'And then, I regretted that I wasted sooooo much time back then,' she laughs.

(b) Don't crib

'Yes, you don't have time. Yeah, life is hard. Yep, we get it, you didn't sleep all night. But you made a choice—stick to it.'

(c) Don't let anyone else waste your time

There will always be people who ask to meet, who want you to take time off for lunch, who grumble that you don't make time for them. 'Ask them to take a hike, if they can't understand your situation. Get out of friendships that cause emotional drama. State in clear terms that there is no more room for drama in your life. Real friends will understand and stick by you.'

Following these rules herself, she found she could take the

time to actually focus on her course of study. She made time for introspection, decided she wanted to switch from the IT industry to brand management, and spoke to her professor about it. She interned with him, and eventually got an enviable job at a reputed company.

Smiling, she says it helped that her husband took over as her minder. 'He took up exactly from where my father left off. If I was chilling out before an exam, he would come and switch off the TV, and ask me to go study. I'd say oh, come on, it's an open book exam, it's case-study based, I want to go out . . . but he would be all like, "What the hell? If I were you, I'd have locked myself up in a room and be studying". Guilt-tripping works.'

A marriage is what one makes of it, Shwetha feels. It's possible to do a lot of things after marriage, but one should be ready to handle the responsibility and the realities that come with it.

'Parents will just try and paint a rosy picture. Your marriage and children are items for them to tick off. They will try and finish of their checklist asap. You need to figure out whether you're ready to run the show, to work towards a happy marriage.'

She doesn't want to frighten people off marriage though. There are entirely good sides to it, such as companionship, especially while travelling. 'My parents were super-worried when I was single and travelling with friends. And though I didn't marry Hulk Hogan, they were somehow under the impression that travelling with my husband was a lot safer!'

Riding the air waves

Aarthi Varanasi explains how she prepared her family and
children for her transition from homemaker to celebrity.

From being a housewife whose cheery conversation and easy wit made her popular in her small circle of friends, Aarthi Varanasi would suddenly become the coolest mum in her children's school. Starting off as a radio jockey at the age of 32, she became a film playback singer, a voiceover artist and emcee over the next few years. Of Telugu origin and raised in Chennai, Aarthi is multilingual, and has found avenues for her vocal talent in both the Tamil and Telugu film industries.

Aarthi was married at 23, right after she had completed her postgraduation. She had her first child the following year, and the second two years after that. There was no time to work. The question of her working had never been broached before or after marriage, and Aarthi had no time to think about it as long as her children were toddlers.

'But once they started going to full-day school, I realized

there is nothing for me to do besides just taking care of them, and I started questioning myself,' she says, 'What am *I* doing? Okay, agreed, I give them food, take care of them, make snacks for them when they come back, spend time with them. But other than that, for those eight hours when I had all the time in the world, what am I doing? Housework will always be there, whether the children are small, grown-up or married. But what am I doing for *myself*? I can sing well, I can talk well.'

Her entry into radio occurred by accident, in 2005. Just as Aarthi was wondering what she should do, Radio Mirchi announced an RJ hunt. She had always been a radio listener, and says she was inspired enough by popular RJs. 'I wanted to be like them, but I had no clue how I was going to become like them.'

When the RJ hunt was announced, she saw an opportunity, but was hesitant. 'At the first interview, I was asked to script an entire, twelve-link show. And I'd never written a single piece of dialogue in my life. Yes, I was a good orator, and I was involved in theatre in school and college, but I'd never done scripting per se. It was only after I wrote that script that I realized I could do this too—I could write well too.'

Even as she was discovering her own potential, other people sensed it. One of the RJs at Mirchi told her she was a natural, another gave her tips, and another taught her how to handle situations where things went wrong. She was selected as one of five finalists, the only woman to have made it as far. That was when she realized she had it in her to make a name for herself.

At this time, family support was a key factor. 'In the last stage of the hunt, we had to do live shows, and that was at night, from 1 a.m. to 6 a.m., when there was no in-studio RJ. Imagine a husband coming back from a long day at work, and saying, "All right, you go, I'll look after the kids." If I didn't have that support, I couldn't have done it. So, I used to take a call-taxi in the middle of the night, while he looked after the children. It was so risky, now that I think of it. But I did it, because I so passionately wanted to do it, I so passionately wanted to make a mark on my own.'

When she lost out in the last round, one of the radio channel's most popular RJs came up to her and said, 'You should have won. I so badly wanted you in. You were brilliant.' She was surprised, flattered and buoyed. Over the next year, she did get calls from the radio station every time there was a vacancy, but things didn't work out. Timings had to be considered too. She had to make sure her work hours coincided with those of her children's school.

'I'd lost all hope. Then, the following year, one of my friends heard that Radio City was being launched and he called up immediately and told me to apply because they were looking for RJs,' she says. 'After the first round itself, my boss told me he saw a bright future for me, and that I was definitely in. That gave me a lot of confidence. He's been in radio for so long, and he says something like that. So, I thought, I need to prove him right, I need to take it up.'

There was a rider, though. She would have to be at office from 7 a.m. to whatever time the work was done. Her boss told her that her family would have to forget she existed, for a month and a half. She would have to slog it out for the next

117

forty-five days to get the station up and running, and only then could he offer her the job of an RJ.

'I came back and told my husband and mother-in-law, "Look, I need your support. If you don't help me, I will be missing out on one of the biggest opportunities of my life." Seriously, not everybody will get a break like that. You're married, you're the mother of two, you've not worked anywhere, you're almost a decade older than the other people applying, and out of nowhere you get a plum offer. My conviction had to be conveyed to them, and it was very difficult. I explained that this was something that I personally needed to do.'

Stepping back from her own specific case, Aarthi says reactions to an announcement of this sort could range from the supportive to hostile. When you marry early, especially in an arranged set-up, certain things are taken for granted. The bride's new family doesn't fully know her personality, and can't guess at the ambitions she may nurse. No one can tell in which direction a woman of 23 will grow over the next few years. It could take her husband by surprise; it could even take her by surprise.

'My husband supported me completely, but you will face a lot of criticism from some quarters. You need to put your foot down. Ultimately, this is your life, your reality, your career. I was very clear about one thing—another four or five years down the line, when my children go to college or boarding school, if I look back and realize I've only raised my children and nothing else, that's not going to give me much satisfaction. Yes, I will be happy that I've raised them well, and given them moral values and taught them tradition. But what have I done for myself? I didn't want to be known as Kumar's daughter and Ravi's wife and Nilan and Pranav's mother. Who am I? Who is Aarthi? What is her identity?'

When she found out she had no answer, she decided she had to go to work. Aarthi gave herself some time to figure out her strengths and weaknesses, and what she could do. Once she had made up her mind, Aarthi says, destiny helped her out. Her boss at Radio City was willing to schedule her hours so that she could leave by 4 p.m.

However, convincing her little children that their mother wasn't going to be at home as much as they were used to was far more difficult than convincing her husband and in-laws.

'Touch wood, I've been blessed with understanding children. They saw that I was really happy. Not that I was unhappy otherwise, but this was an altogether different rush. Of course, despite all this, there will be resistance. They were really small. You need to make them understand, to make them feel important, to make them feel responsible. So I would explain to them that if Amma goes to a job, she can do so much more for you all. I would ask their permission. It was never, "Amma is going out." It was, "Kanna [darling], Amma has to go out, will you help Amma?" Every mother has to give the children that respect, show them you're not doing this without consulting them. You need to be honest with them. They're mature enough to understand. If you lie and say you're doing this only for them, they will say they don't want this, and rebel. I told them I was happier working. I would explain where I was going and why, and when I would come back, and whether there would be a delay, and if so, why. You shouldn't hide anything from them.'

Despite all this, Aarthi had her share of tantrums and heartbreaks to deal with. When her son, who was just over five years old at the time, fell ill, he would cry and ask her to stay behind. Sometimes, they would stop by her office on the way back from school, hoping to pick her up. As an RJ, it wasn't easy to take days off work—she not only had her dedicated listeners, but finding a stand-in was impossible. All the RJs were on contract, and came in only for the hours that their show covered.

'At these times, you think, "Oh, my God, why did I do this? Is my job more important than my children? Is this money more important?" These things *will* occur to you. But you have to get past all those hurdles. It's a very difficult balance, and it does put a lot of pressure on the person who's doing it. When you work, to kill your guilt over not spending time with the children, sometimes you go overboard with getting gifts for them or giving in to their wants. That was something I did initially, and then I realized that I should not do it.'

The hardest part of going to work, as a mother, was understanding when the children really needed her, and when they were simply feeling insecure and needed reassurance. It's a fine line to tread, Aarthi says, but it's important to be strong and stick to one's career.

'But having said that, you should always keep in mind that the family is the base,' she adds. The onus is on the mother to keep the family in harmony. 'If you realize that you're breaking your family harmony to work, there's something wrong with *you*. You need to make sure you balance things. There will always be problems, and you need to figure out ways to handle them—what if you have an important meeting when one of the children is sick? At every stage, it is a challenge.'

There were times when she would give them medicine, rush to office, and call up every hour with instructions to whoever was at home. If her husband was in town, he would work out of home when the children took ill. If he was travelling, her mother-in-law would step in. Her parents also live in the same city, and so they could step in too.

'Even so, you feel so guilty, so bad, thinking about your baby at home wanting you. You keep questioning yourself, asking if your need to have a life of your own is worth all this, asking whether your career is more important than your children. You need to grit your teeth and get past those weak moments.'

It helped that many of the other mothers at her children's school were going back to work, too. Several had taken some years off work to look after their children. Some had gone right back to their jobs after a few months' maternity leave. Soon, Aarthi's children realized their mother had a cooler job than most.

'They were so proud of me,' she says fondly. 'They told everyone in school about their mother being a radio jockey. Once, the Principal came up to me and told me she'd heard I was an RJ, and that's so cool.'

The children quickly settled into a routine of looking after themselves, under their grandmother's supervision. If Aarthi wasn't yet home when they came back from school, they would change their clothes, have their milk, and go out to play. If they had exams, she would often be pleasantly surprised to see them studying on their own.

'And now, even when they're ill, they ask me to go out if something comes up. They encourage me to do my own thing. Sometimes, they say, "You go, Amma, don't think about us, you go for a holiday, enjoy yourself, you have a life of your own." They're very mature, and I think that comes when you give them that independence.'

However, Aarthi warns that independence is a tricky thing. Children can easily misuse their freedom, and all working mothers need to be wary of it. 'You *have* to know what's happening in their lives, and for this, you have to be more their friend than their mother.' However tired a working mother is, she has to make time to exchange stories with her children at the end of the day.

Sorting out her family's routine was only one of the demands of going back to work. Aarthi, at 32, was joining an industry which was dominated by people right out of college. Tamil radio is closely linked to the film industry, and RJs regularly interview film personalities. Often, they become friends. Many young people see this as an opportunity to enter the film world, as singers as well as actors, and are willing to work for lower salaries than older people. Besides, radio is seen as a vibrant, peppy medium that should stay young. Some radio channels don't hire RJs who are over 25.

'Luckily in my case, Radio City only looked at my voice and talent, not my age, my career graph, or how many children

I had,' she says, 'I was honest about it. But I was only told that I would have to work long hours, and that I would need to relate to my audience. Everything else was cool.'

She made an effort to think like the audience. She would speak to the teenagers she knew. She did her homework. She followed comedy channels so that she could keep up with the latest catchphrases and punchlines in cinema. She would read the papers and browse the internet to keep herself updated on what the trends were.

'The most important thing is to compartmentalize your life. You're a mother at home. When you come to work, you're an RJ and your job is to make your listeners relate to you, to make sense to them. I never worried about whether I was too old for the job, and I had the sort of ambience at work that helped me feel young. My colleagues and I would have so much fun, we would do the sort of crazy stuff you do back in college, but at the same time we'd work hard and make sure we got good results.'

The other issue Aarthi had to deal with was the disparity between her salary and those of her friends from school and college, who had married later than she had, or not married yet.

'On the flipside, that was one of the things that got me thinking about going back to work,' she says. 'But initially, it was difficult.' She had to tell herself to keep the faith, to realize that in a few months, she would grow, and she would get her salary hikes, and that she would make money from the allied fields her job gave her access to—playback singing and emceeing.

'But whatever your starting salary is, you feel *so* good just being able to swipe your own credit card and buying yourself or your children something when you're out shopping, without having to consult your husband. That financial independence gives you a lot of confidence. And I tell you, people treat you with more respect when you're a working woman. I think it's a lot of bullshit when people say they don't set store by it. When you lose your "housewife" tag, people are scared to say some things, they hesitate to be rude.'

And, for herself, the satisfaction of doing something in addition to cooking and running a house is something that can't be expressed in words, Aarthi says. 'Being a good wife and mother is a very difficult job. And to have a life apart from that, in which you're not just making money, but also exposing your own talent, it gives you a big thrill. That is a feeling nobody can take away from you. You feel younger, you feel more energetic. The other day, I met someone who asked how old my kids are, and she was shocked when I said they're 14 and 12. She was like, "I thought you'd have one 4- or 5-year-old. This is amazing!"'

Her Santoor moments aside, Aarthi feels working has also taught her to get over a certain mindset that makes women feel they belong with their children. 'We're born like that, it's deeply embedded in us, and we not only put family first, we feel constantly guilty when we're not at home. Of late, I see some women who put themselves first, or give themselves as much importance, at least. But why do you think there are so many women who give up their careers, after a few years, when their children are entering their teens? There are so many software professionals who stop working because the children need their mothers' attention. Of course, there are certain circumstances which can lead you to make that decision, and it should be respected. But my point is that it sometimes doesn't occur to us that we're entitled to lives of our own.'

Aarthi stresses that women, even if they marry young, should not be limited by husband, family and children. 'Marriage is not the be-all and end-all of life. Some women think family *is* their life. You need to think beyond. The minute you draw boundaries for yourself, the minute you're satisfied with your life, you're not going to grow. You should never be satisfied. You should be dissatisfied, in the sense you should have your own targets, and you should aim at constantly outgrowing yourself, let alone others. You compete with others at a later stage; first, you have to compete with yourself and not be the same. You need to evolve, to change. Who I was ten years ago, I can't be now. What mistakes I made ten years ago, I can't make now.'

It was this thought that made Aarthi decide that she wouldn't give up working, as she had done ten years earlier in order to get married. And now, as her children listen to the songs she has sung, and her friends know her not just as 'Mrs Varanasi' but as 'RJ Aarthi', she knows she made the right decision in reinventing herself.

When it all crumbles

Preethi Madhavan speaks about getting married for the wrong reasons, how to recognize when a marriage is not working, why it's so hard to take the final call to get a divorce, and why one should walk out of a bad marriage.

When a relationship doesn't work out, we all know what we do—take a break, introspect, maybe cheat, and then call it off. In a marriage, it isn't so simple. There are the fat wedding albums, the memories of shared stresses, the hungry relatives searching for scraps of scandal, the terrified parents and the stigma of the label of 'divorcee'.

No one walks into a marriage on the assumption that it will end, but it's a bad idea to get into one for reasons such as, 'I'm so bloody sick of the groom hunt!', or 'Pah, people will finally stop asking me when they can eat at my wedding!', or 'I need to get away from my parents!' To begin with, it isn't the end of the questions, as much as the start of a whole lot of new questions and pressures. 'When are you going to have a baby? It's not easy to conceive, you know. It gets harder after 30.' 'You should have a second child. Only children are lonely, and they grow up selfish.' 'You look haggard. Is everything okay at home?' But, all the questions aside, one is never prepared for marriage until one is married.

Software professional Preethi Madhavan, who is now 30, was to find out devastatingly that she'd entered wedlock for all the wrong reasons. Her parents had been searching for grooms for four years, and she was tired of meeting a line of men with fancy degrees, whose biggest concern was whether she was a virgin or not, whether she'd had boyfriends or not, and how far she'd gone with each of them, and whether she was still in touch with any.

'Once I met this guy, who was an IIT *and* IIM alumnus, and he said something along the lines of, "If I figure out my wife is not a virgin, I will beat her out of the house",' she recalls with a laugh. 'I was like, "Namaskaaram. May you find a masochist."'

But encounters of this sort had damaged her morale, psyche and clear-headedness. The final straw was a bitter experience. She'd finally met a man she genuinely liked, and to top it off, the horoscopes matched. They'd met several times over four months, and decided to get married. His parents were to come down to formalize the engagement, and her parents had taken the horoscopes back to the astrologer, to figure out an auspicious date. But the astrologer had suddenly exclaimed, 'Oh, my God, this is all wrong. The horoscopes don't match at all!'

To Preethi's horror, her parents decided not to 'risk it'. And worse, her soon-to-be-fiancé chickened out too, saying his parents set a lot of store by horoscopes.

'I was just so angry. And so tired of everything,' Preethi says, 'On top of this, an aunt I was really close to was dying. There were too many tragedies in my life, and I wanted to escape my parents as quickly as possible, because they just kept parking one guy after another in front of me.'

She was complaining about her situation to Raja, a good friend of hers. Raja was also Malayali, and his parents had also been scouting for a match for him. They would meet, and laugh about the horrors they met.

'At the time, my parents were after me to marry this guy with a PhD in a subject so vague and random and putting-off that I was like, "No way in hell can I even *speak* to this guy",' she says. 'And he had come down from the US, and was waiting for me to say yes. And once I did, we'd be engaged within a week or something. So, I was telling Raja how sick I was of everything, and how I was going to tell my parents that I'm not getting married for three years.'

And Raja responded with arguably the worst proposal in history. 'My parents are also looking out for someone, so you tell me, if it works for you, we can think about something. Like, maybe getting married, you know. At least we know each other.'

Preethi was initially taken aback, but she knew he was that kind of guy— practical, unromantic and safe. The basis on which they got into the marriage had the same pragmatism in it—they were friends, they belonged to compatible castes, so why not take it to the next level?

'We have to recognize that there is a type of a middle thing as well, that is arranged by you,' she says. 'Not the dramatic sort of love story where your parents are opposing it; not the happy love story where the parents agree and you have a traditional marriage; not the purely arranged marriage, where your friends or parents or relatives pick a stranger out for you, and you interact for some time and marry. There is another category, of people who already know each other, and are not in love per se, but think there's some potential, an interesting friendship that could become a more lasting relationship. So you don't enter that relationship with the notion of being in love or romance or anything. It's calculated.'

She now recognizes that neither of them was in the right mindset for marriage, and that would shake its foundation.

They had an eight-month-long engagement, but even though she knew they would be marrying each other, she could never bring herself to love him in any way other than as a friend. She assumed the relationship would change after marriage, and it did, but not in the manner she expected. But before we get to that, there's another tricky aspect to converting a friendship into a relationship— where does the chemistry come from?

Can anyone build chemistry?

Preethi admits that it's difficult, and one needs to be wary of how easily one can be fooled into imagining chemistry. She assumed love, and chemistry, would grow on them. They did have a deep friendship, and even now, separated and waiting for their divorce to come through, they want each other to be happy, she says. But it simply didn't work in a marriage.

'Friendship is a good foundation, but you need to build on it—and before that, you need to get some other basics right.

Marriage is about two completely different people coming together, and becoming a unit in some senses. In our case, our personalities were very dissimilar, and also, our environment wasn't conducive to a marriage.'

She feels it's important to bloom in a relationship, to feel one is being nourished, and that one's partner is also growing because of their bond.

She identifies four levels of compatibility:

- ❖ **Physical:** A couple should be able to harmoniously share the same spaces, should feel a sense of attraction when they are together. Sometimes, you just fit. If you don't *fit in* when you're making love, if there's a sense of unease, of awkwardness not only in the closeness, but in the sense that the dimensions feel all wrong, that the couple feels strangely disconnected, an essential element is lacking.

- ❖ **Emotional:** A couple should connect at a deeper level, where they understand each other's emotions, beyond words. One could say, 'Leave me alone', when one means, 'I need you, but I don't want to admit it', or 'Persuade me that I don't want to be alone'. The other needs to sense it, and to be willing to indulge one when one needs it most.

- ❖ **Intellectual:** What keeps a couple's chemistry alive is being challenged intellectually every day, especially if both are intellectually inclined. There shouldn't be a sense of competitiveness, but each must feel the partner is pushing him or her a little bit, to be his or her best, to grow a little bit. Of course, it also means the couple should ideally share an interest in several fields, or be willing to understand each other's fields.

❖ **Spiritual:** This is the most important, that a married couple finds spiritual compatibility. It doesn't necessarily have to do with religion. It may have to do with existential concerns, or with the big questions that trouble one.

'The spiritual aspect is completely missing in most marriages these days,' Preethi says. 'Even if you're able to hit the first two levels—physical and emotional—it's a big deal. I think, when the concept of marriage came in, it had not only to do with companionship and reproduction, keeping the human race alive, but for that sort of compatibility, that resonance.'

The breakdown

One of the main reasons Preethi decided to marry Raja was that a sense of equality had always been crucial to her. She, like most people, believed one's partner should also be one's best friend. And that, she feels, derives from a sense of equality, of trust, of understanding. Things needed to be transparent and open. If she had a crush on someone else, she needed to be able to joke about it with her husband. If she caught him checking a woman out, she needed to be able to tease him about it. That was what their friendship had been like, and things didn't change much during their courtship.

But when they got married, things changed drastically, and that took her by surprise. Perhaps it was that he knew too much—whom she'd dated, whom she'd slept with, what her views were. He became strangely possessive.

'These roles are assumed,' she says. 'It's like, "Now, I'm your husband, now I shall not allow you to speak to this man", or "Why is this person calling you up all the time?", or "Why does he call up at this time of night?" All these filters start coming in.'

And the assumption of roles affected her in other ways. When she moved into his home, she discovered a completely new person. When they had been friends, and even during their engagement, Raja had been the kind who would volunteer to help out with things. When he came home, he would help her make the tea. He would take the initiative when things needed to be done around the house. He would follow her mother to the kitchen and chat away. But at home, he was different.

'In four and a half years, I don't think he's once got into the kitchen and made tea. He'd expect the tea to come to him, he'd expect the breakfast to come to him, irrespective of what time he woke up,' Preethi said. 'That was a shock. And maybe because we lived with his parents, and that was how his mother had raised him and she thought it was completely normal, the entire family thought this was the course of things. As much as you have interacted with a person outside, when you get into their own comfort zones, their own environments, you will definitely make new, new, new, new discoveries that you have to take one at a time. And they are often unpleasant.'

Living with the in-laws

Preethi, like many women of her generation, lived with her in-laws after marriage. Sometimes it's a question of convenience, when both members of the couple work. Sometimes, it has to do with staving off the insecurities of parents who feel abandoned when their sons leave their homes. Either way it's a bad idea, she feels.

'For any woman, when you're newly married, when you're entering a different life, you want to make a home, you want to choose the furniture and curtains, the crockery and cutlery, the mugs, the walls, you dream of painting walls together, arguing over colours. You want to build your home, and it becomes a metaphor for the process of the growth of the relationship. You walk into an empty house, and you fill it with something together. You bring the best things into your home, the things you like, the things you find beautiful, the things that comfort you, your little idiosyncrasies. And you do it all together—and it's so important, especially in your first year of marriage, to build those rituals.'

As an example, she tells the story of a couple she knows who have two children and live in a joint family. They've followed one ritual every day, since the day they got married. Every morning, at 8.30, they walk down to a tea shop at the end of the road where they live, have a cup of tea, have their own conversation in their alone time, and come back. It takes all of ten minutes, but it's one of those small things that can be immensely important in keeping a marriage together, in making one feel harboured, in making one feel one isn't alone.

'If these rituals get broken, you feel the rupture in your relationship. You've built something, and then you can't sustain it. In Raja's and my case, we struggled even to build something. We couldn't come up with a single ritual in all those years. We thought we'd go out for dinner every Friday, but something or the other would come up. The point of a ritual is, whatever the crisis, whatever happens, you do it. It's a way of saying, "At this time, I'll be there, no matter what. We're together in this."'

The fact that there was no 'their thing', and the fact that she had walked into a house that already had its routines made her feel unanchored.

'When I went to my parents' home, to the one I had grown up in, I never felt like I was home. And when I went to Raja's house, I didn't feel like I was at home either—yes, it was my house now, and I knew I was part of the family, but I never felt like it was my *home*, because there was no creation of mine, or of ours together, in it. So, that makes a huge difference.'

The clinginess of parents can be debilitating to a marriage.

'It happens a lot nowadays, surprisingly so, and by the way most of these people are the ones who've walked out on their own parents, for other cities, for other jobs, for whatever reason,' she points out, laughing at the irony. 'Most of that generation lived away from parents. They'd go look in on them maybe once a year. Many of them were not present even when the parents died. But, somehow, when it comes to their sons, there is an expectation of a joint family, which I feel is completely unfair. *They* had the luxury of space to build their lives, raise their children. Why not give it to us?'

In Preethi's case, the fact that they lived with her in-laws meant she had a four-hour commute to work—two hours each way. She would leave the house at 7 a.m. and return at 10 p.m. She felt guilty about not being able to help her mother-in-law with work around the house. Weekends were her only reprieve, and so she was too tired to do anything around the house.

She feels there's another aspect to the clinginess—it is yet another instance of parents giving their children a shield, saving them from the responsibilities of running a house. As a culture, she feels, India keeps people irresponsible—and submissive—for too long.

Whose money is our money?

Another issue Preethi was unprepared for was the idea of shared finances. She had always handled her money and investments, though her parents didn't think much of her financial acumen. When Raja and she decided to get married, he suggested they open a joint account.

'Many times, especially if you've been friends, you go in with a lot of trust, which is good actually. But I think you need to keep yourself safe as well, and these contracts of money, and understanding, should be drawn right away.'

Neither of them had individual savings once they got married—they had one account, which was handled by the husband. Most of the money in that account was going into his home loan, a loan he had taken to buy the house they lived in. It had been a good investment, and the house was worth something in the range of Rs 3 crore now, far more than the price they had bought it for. Raja had a weakness for gadgets, and since the EMI for the loan was high, he ran up a credit card debt. He took personal loans to settle the debt, getting into further debt.

When Preethi finally decided to walk out of the marriage, she was told there was only Rs 2000 in the joint account. She had no savings, since all her money was going into it. And she was asked to sign over control of the account to her husband, and withdraw her name from it.

'Yes, I was a fool. It's foolishness. I don't even know if he had the intention of fooling me or cheating me, or whatever. It was just circumstantial. He moved the money, and that goes back to this change in equation—the man feels that he owns her, so owns her money, he owns her things, he has the liberty to move her things, he has the liberty to use her money. That's what you need to be wary of. So, all right, you two are a unit. But shouldn't you give each other that amount of respect? If you're going to move her money, shouldn't you ask her or keep her informed at least? It's *our* money, right? But the lines start blurring.'

She feels the best way out is to have a joint account, but also have separate savings accounts. A percentage of earnings goes into the joint account. That way, you're not paying for a house that will never be yours.

Preethi is now in a happy, live-in relationship. Can an arranged marriage achieve that sort of harmony?

She finds the question difficult to answer. One way of looking at it, of course, is that there are different ways of meeting a person—whether you run into him at a concert, or you work together, or you meet online, or you meet through friends, or you meet through family. An arranged marriage could simply be another way of meeting a man you fall in love with. But, she says, a marriage only really starts when you're married. Even when two people are dating, they're putting on masks at times—pretending to like things they don't, pretending to be better people than they are, camouflaging their eccentricities.

But, of course, there's a huge difference. When you're dating someone you've met by chance, you don't know how long the relationship will last, you don't know whether he's the marrying kind, you don't know what he's keeping from you, you don't know whether you'll sleep with him. When you meet someone with the idea of marriage already on both your minds, and your family waiting like a wake of vultures, everything is more rushed.

'You know, I feel it's like plucking a fruit before it's completely ripe. It's like those artificial injections you put in to ripen them faster!' Preethi says. There isn't enough time to get comfortable with someone, so you take up a checklist, and tick off whatever answer appears most suited to your preferences.

Unprepared for responsibility

Preethi says parents need to be more responsible about their children's marriages—it isn't a duty they can tick off a list, it's a responsibility to their children. One of the reasons for the increasing rate of divorces, she feels, is parental pressure in the face of the unpreparedness of children.

'In the end, what do parents want for their children? They want them to be happy, right? But they take away the wrong responsibilities, and impose the wrong ones.'

The problem starts when parents say, 'We've found this person for you, this person is perfect, all you have to do is marry him, and your life will be fine'. This essentially means the parents have taken on all responsibility for the rest of the life of the child. But once the daughter is married, the marriage becomes her responsibility—a burden she is unprepared for.

'In Indian society, children are never given the opportunity to take on responsibility. That is the biggest problem with marriages. Why are Indian youngsters so confused about marriage? Because they're trained to not take responsibility for the longest period of time. School—your parents decide which school you go to. College—they decide what stream you choose. Suddenly, when *you* have to choose a person, which is probably a lifetime's decision, is when all the confusions erupt. Because now you have to take on some responsibility. Even if your parents have chosen the guy, they're not going to stand behind you and instruct you every day. Even if they do, in ten years, they'll both die. So, you have to live your life anyway. Then you're also participating in taking on that responsibility, and that's why most youngsters are freaked out by the idea of marriage, especially arranged ones.'

Why are marriages so hard to break?

Preethi answers with a single, poignant word—hope. She knew six months into her marriage that it was not going the right way. But she stuck it out for the next four years, because the decision was too tough. She could have stayed on in the marriage, and no one would have known it wasn't working, except she and Raja.

'It was definitely the choice between "Do I want to live my

life more openly?" and "Do I live a life where everything seems perfect, but I am not at peace inside?" Either you get out of it, and break everything that exists, or you live inside it and break yourself. You want to survive through this marriage, and you want to show the society that you're married, and your parents will be happy that you're married. But at some point, you have to realize it doesn't work. Somewhere, the marriage has failed, it's become a farce. You could stay on in it, and have children, and they may not know how unhappy you are. Or, you could leave it, which is, of course, healthier for you. But it takes a long time to work up the strength to leave it.'

'The arranged marriage set-up is like speed dating'

Devyani Khanna, whose family has been looking for a match, speaks about the things that are wrong with the arranged marriage set-up, and how one can cope with this framework.

There are those who strike a match right away, either from instinct or from careful filtering, or from the inability to refuse. And then there are those who spend years trying to find partners, and grow demoralized as each encounter leaves a worse taste in the mouth. In my own case, the question of arranged marriage would be brought up every time a relative or family friend asked whether I was 'available'. If I was in a relationship, the question would be hedged. If I wasn't, I would be consulted. Since, until recently, I wasn't sure whether I would be willing to give an arranged marriage a shot, I would shrug my shoulders and the process would be set in motion.

I've never met any of the prospects in person, but rejected

two on the basis of appearance—yes, women do that too—and rejected two more on the basis of accent and conversational skills after speaking to them on the phone. These four set-ups were spaced out over seven years, and after the last I announced that I didn't see the point in arranged marriage—not when the criteria for shortlists included caste, height, education and horoscopes. I've often wondered about how women who are as picky as I am—which many women are—continue to keep the faith, how they push themselves to meet one groom after the other.

Devyani Khanna, 27, has worked in event management in Delhi and Mumbai. Her family has been looking for a groom for her for about three years, and she acknowledges that the process can be frustrating and exhausting.

'It's important to take breaks. You never meet one after the other. It's not easy. Sometimes, it is very depressing, very heartbreaking, disappointing, hard. But this is what you need to ask yourself—do you see yourself *meeting* anybody? I don't. I'm very sure that I don't want to be with someone from my industry, or even a related one, like media. So, that's ruled out, and the only way to meet someone is through the parents. You have to push yourself, and after a bad experience you have to really *drag* yourself to meet the next person. But also remember that you need to be open and willing to let people into your life. So, if you sense that you're shutting down, there's no point; take a break. You may miss a really good offer because you're not in the mood, but anyway, you won't realize it's a good offer when you're that unmotivated.'

She points out that it's not pleasant to keep meeting and

141

talking to strangers. It can leave one feeling emotionally drained. 'That's a huge negative in an arranged marriage, because it can make you doubt your own self, make you doubt whether there is anybody out there who is meant for you, because you meet all sorts of strange people and you have strange experiences. At first, you laugh about it with your friends, but eventually, when you get more serious, you just feel . . . like, *what the hell*, you know.'

The approach

Devyani has learnt to identify certain parameters that she uses as filters to decide whether she even wants to meet someone. When she started out, she had a checklist. However, she says, over these crucial years, her priorities have changed and her personality has evolved. Now, she trusts her instinct. Her main concerns are in line with those of her family. She will meet a man if he is:

❖ well-settled
❖ well-educated
❖ from a respectable family

Once those three factors have been ticked off, she discards the checklist when she goes for a meeting. 'Each year, as you're finding a partner, you meet a few people. So, as you have new experiences, your choices are evolving, your expectations are evolving. Now, I base my decisions on how I feel with a person, whether he can make me laugh, how he treats me, whether I feel comfortable, things like that. I think it has to do with the age group. At 24−25, things like "Is he a reader? Is he tall? Is he handsome?" were important to me. Now, all that is secondary.'

She says the years between 24−25 and 27−29 are formative years in a woman's life. It's the gap during which we figure out what we are, what we want from life, and whom we want to spend it with.

'At 24−25, you're just out of college, or you've worked for a year or two, depending on how much you've studied. You haven't figured out enough about yourself. At the time, you're still very influenced by what society thinks, what family thinks. If your parents feel a guy is nice, you will be affected by it, though what they're looking for is different from what you're looking for. And when you rebel, you rebel for the wrong reasons. Say, if a guy is extremely good-looking but not well-educated, we'd be so floored by his looks that we may make a decision we will regret later.'

There is another side to it. Devyani agrees that a 24-year-old just *may* mould herself according to her partner, but she feels one needs to be at least 27 to make a sensible decision and not get carried away by extraneous factors.

That said, the decision to marry depends on conditioning. It may have less to do with age than time spent in the marriage circuit. 'In my case, my family only got to talking about it when I was around 24. So now I've reached the stage where I'm totally prepared for marriage, and I know what to look for. Then again, some women are conditioned by the age of 20 to expect that they will be looking for husbands right out of college, and will be married by 24. So, they too, have spent the same three or four years thinking about it, and maybe they're as prepared. That's assuming they don't find partners immediately. It's possible, of course, and I don't think 20−21 is anywhere *close* to the right age for marriage.'

The right to ask for what you want

In an arranged marriage set-up, too many things are dismissed as shallow. Often, they are the very things that lead us to fall in love or—in a less ideal situation—to get attracted to someone. These are things like looks, accent, pronunciation, manners and upbringing. While people aren't always looking for partners who could be runway models, they do need to find something appealing about a partner. Right?

Devyani concurs with this view. 'You know, I look at things like the way a person talks, his accent, his pronunciation and his sense of chivalry. What I've been told is that I shouldn't be nitpicking, but those small things do put me off, so I've not applied that to myself so far. I wonder whether I *should* look beyond all that sometimes, but I don't think I will be happy with a man who doesn't have these things in place.'

To some of us, things like hygiene and demeanour are important, and it's okay for that not to change. Yes, there is compromise in a marriage, but one needn't condemn oneself to a pigsty. 'One of the things that bother me so much is—what if my husband is not polished? What if he isn't clean?' Devyani says, 'And in an arranged set-up, where do you find the comfort level to tell him something that personal? And by then, won't he say, "You were okay with it all along, what happened now?" So if a man picks his nose, scratches parts of his body, or does anything else that one finds repulsive, one should know things won't click.'

She's quick to add that 'clicking' doesn't mean there should be fireworks and raging chemistry. 'It's just that the guy should not say anything untoward, and the meeting should be pleasant. People do talk all sorts of nonsense. Like once, I had a very odd experience. I met this guy who was an IIM graduate. And he was giving me all this random shit about how the moment he'd passed out of IIM, girls were flocking over to him and begging him to marry them. And then he gave me some even more judgmental crap. He said, "I know you Mumbai–Delhi type girls are not narrow-minded, but now this has spread over to small-town girls also. Everyone has boyfriends, they've lost their moral values." Then, without any connection to anything else, he said, "I don't want someone who just earns 30,000–40,000 a month, I want a real professional." I felt like every second sentence was exploding in my head. And finally, he went, "You let me know, because girls only have the choice nowadays." I wanted to tell him I'd made my choice half an hour ago.'

The filters

So, where even education doesn't come with guarantees, Devyani set up her filters. 'All right, so you find out there can be really stupid people from IIT or IIM. Being Indian, of course, you expect some level of sophistication from them. First, there was the Moral Values guy, and then there was one more who called me up, and went, "Are you free, kya?" "Based in Mumbai, kya?" I'm like . . . Whaaat? *Whaaat?* How can you throw a "kya" into every sentence?!'

She figured out that one of the things the two had in common, aside from the IIM tag, was their small-town upbringing. 'I'm not saying small-town people are not nice, but you're very unlikely to be able to ever relate to them, unless you're from a small town too. These are people who haven't gone out of their Lucknow, or some little village, until they did their engineering. Frankly, they'll never be able to match up to your level of thinking. Even if they've travelled the world, gone to IIT or IIM, whatever, if they've spent their entire lives in that little town, they won't have the extra zing that you look for. Of course, there could be all sorts of people out there, but this has been my experience so far.'

Devyani put down a couple of ground rules, 'to save myself from all these losers':

❖ Never go to meet a small-town person
❖ Never meet someone who asks you to a coffee shop

'Let me explain the coffee shop thing a bit. Places like Barista and Costa are perfectly nice places to meet friends. But if I were a guy, I would not ask to meet a woman I am thinking of marrying in places like that. I would like to go to an exclusive coffee shop, in a luxury hotel, where one can talk. Because you know how crowded these Barista-like places are, music is playing, and everyone is staring at you—they all know you may be meeting for the first time, because you're yelling over the noise, telling the other person where you grew up, what you did, what you like and so on. They're trying to eavesdrop to see what you're talking about. You know, you often see these people, and you find it really funny. I don't want to be one of those.'

She feels hotels are quieter, people aren't staring at the other tables, and the ambience is a little more conducive to actually talking. 'It also reassures me that they're on the same wavelength as me, and also of the same social class. I know these aren't the politically correct things to say, but they do matter. It's not like my family eats three times a day in a five-star hotel, but going to one isn't a big deal either. Especially when it's something this crucial, you shouldn't be thinking about why you must pay a few hundred rupees more for a five-star coffee. It's worth it because it's not some place where people are dumping stuff on the table, and interrupting to ask how the food is, and waiting for you to leave. The whole atmosphere changes, and you feel different about it. It shows you that the guy is serious too.'

Then, of course, there are the obvious gauges. If a man doesn't insist on picking up the cheque on a pseudo-date, clearly he's not the sort of man you want to live with, if chivalry is important to you. 'Once, a guy expected me to pay, and after that I've got so paranoid, I don't even offer any more—which is quite rude on my part. And that I don't even pretend to go Dutch may put a guy off. These are the things you need to get over.'

The bug in the system

While ground rules are good to have, Devyani says it's important to be practical about things. When you're choosing a partner to spend the rest of your life with, you can't simply go by pointers. And what she finds exasperating about the process is the superficiality of it. 'It has no depth, I don't know if there is any scope for getting to know a person.'

'The ambience has changed. You don't have two families pretending to make conversation while you're sitting in the next room with a stranger who is just as awkward as you, with fifteen minutes to arrive at a consensus on whether to get married or not. Sometimes, the families don't even meet each other before the couple do. But the attitude hasn't changed,' Devyani says.

You get half an hour, or forty minutes, during which you and your prospective spouse are judging each other's every word and every move. 'You have only those forty minutes to impress and be impressed. And there is so much more to that person, and you're never going to get to know that if you're not *impressed* in that time. See, the other guy may have had a bad day, and he's tired or groggy. And he's just trying to make conversation, and it's not as interesting as you wanted it to be, so you're just going to think "Oh, this guy's so boring", and you won't even give him a second chance. I've done that myself. And I think, to have to judge so quickly is very, very unfair. But it's part of the arranged marriage system. It's like speed dating, only with your family watching and waiting for results.'

The reason people hesitate to give anyone a second chance is that, despite reassurances from modern-day parents, the pressure does build with every meeting. 'When you say yes, he was nice, you're not saying yes to marriage. But both parents start thinking ah, good, it's happening when you're really only saying yes to a second meeting because there's *potential*.

Everyone's decided it's going somewhere, and every time there's more pressure. Third time, though, it's like "ho hi gaya", and fourth time, it's roka.'

This is the factor that makes most people dubious about arranged marriages. You could date a man for years, have met him literally hundreds of times, and yet find something about him that takes you aback, that is a deal-breaker. Place against this the formula for an arranged marriage, according to which one must visualize a future from a couple of meetings in which each partner presents a cobbled-together version of everything that is desirable about him or her.

'This really has to change. There are perfectly good people out there, looking for partners. People who've led normal lives, who've dated, who know what they want. But with the baggage that comes with a pucca arranged marriage, two people—who are really normal, really nice, really good for each other—can crumble under the pressure. You *can't* make up your mind that quickly. Parents will always tell you it's up to you. But, if in the second or third meeting, you realize it's not going anywhere and you pull out, at least one family gets a shock. You'll be blamed and cursed, and told you've led the guy on. And it's worse if a guy does this. I think the way it's structured now, there are still too many disadvantages.'

The solution may be casual set-ups, where people are introduced and allowed to date. Devyani says it works better when couples have been set up through friends, with no 'adults' involved. 'Everyone knows it's a set-up, but they can be relaxed because all that baggage isn't there. No one is going to be calling up anyone else to find out what you said. At the most, your mutual friend may be an intermediary. But in a proper arranged marriage set-up, you have the guy's family calling up the girl, the girl's family calling up his parents, a mediator speaking to both . . . it's too much. People need to chill out a bit about this.'

The logic behind this, she feels, is that it prevents heartbreak. At another level, it is seen as more sensible when one is thinking with one's mind, and not letting one's heart dictate the course of action. Of course, this also means all emotion is cut out of it, and it turns into a business deal. But it's impossible to cut out emotion from human beings. While the emotion in question may not be love, a meeting can leave one feeling angry, humiliated and frustrated. It takes time to calibrate oneself to someone else's sense of humour, to find out what the other person's tastes are, and the marriage market doesn't allow for this. One may take offence at a statement from a stranger that one may find funny coming from a friend or colleague. And when two people are already under some stress, it gets worse.

Devyani warns that there is another insidious process that is set in motion, in an arranged marriage set-up. The norms of eligibility, set by 'society', necessitate a certain level of pretence, of lies.

'For example, I met this guy, whose profile said he was non-vegetarian, and an occasional drinker, but that he doesn't smoke. But when I went in there, he was smelling of smoke, like he'd *just* had a cigarette and come to meet me. I rejected him, because I don't like the idea of someone lying like that. My point is that he could have been open about it. But when I thought back to it later, I realized you *can't* be open about it.

It's just not possible in an arranged marriage set-up, because even if you want to be honest, your parents will feel it makes them look bad. You don't *say* some things even if you *do* some things.'

When you're not even allowed to be honest about yourself, it becomes even harder to know what each person is looking for, and even tougher to connect.

'The thing is, you do evolve, and so it also depends on when you meet somebody. You may meet someone whom you have nothing in common with at the time, but whom you'll recall two years later and think, "Oh, he *would* have been so perfect for me now." That comes with the territory. But I think, at 27–28, you've figured out more or less what you want.'

And at this stage, what one really wants from a partner is acceptance of who one is, and accommodation of who one may become. Because of the way the system is structured, it's hard to get this right the first time. 'The most heartbreaking aspect of an arranged marriage is the pretence you're forced to put on. You never get to know the real person until you're married. You don't get to know the person unless the charade impresses you. You may not be the sort of person who likes to dress up, but you are forced to dress up. The guy may not be a talkative guy, but if he doesn't talk, then he has no chance of being accepted. This judging business is sad, and I don't want to pretend to be somebody, and I don't want that person to pretend to be someone else either, but everyone does in an arranged set-up.'

The corollary of putting on a charade is that one starts living the correct life, the eligible life. Devyani says she has been wanting to get blue and pink streaks in her hair, and she's wanted to do this little experiment since college. However, office regulations wouldn't allow it. Now, she's on a sabbatical, but groom-hunting regulations will not allow for it.

'It's not about how everyone wants a traditional girl. That's not true. But because of the speed-judging, and the fact that you have to bring out who you are in the first impression, you can't act on an impulse. To me, this is a crazy little thing I've been wanting to do. But to a guy I'm meeting, it's evidence that I'm a punk freak. He's going to think I have a bunch of tattoos on my body. And he may *want* someone like that. But that's not me. So that would be a charade too. Now I don't know whether I'll ever get to do the streaks-in-my-hair thing. The most frustrating part of this is the pressure to be eligible— as in, you have to be living that life, and dressing that way, and behaving that way, and appearing that way, just so you become more and more and more and more eligible for the marriage market.'

With a laugh, Devyani recounts a story she heard from a man she met, about his last experience with a prospective wife. Apparently, the girl came in with a questionnaire in her head. As soon as the hi-hello part was done with, she had asked him about his views on miniskirts. A few rapid-fire rounds later, she had got as far as the number of children, and what sort of education they would have. She had wanted to know if he was open to sending them to boarding school, and he'd finally said, 'I don't think I want to entertain such questions.'

'I was laughing so hard, I was like you have to be joking!' Devyani says. 'I mean, what kind of girl asks things like that of a man she's meeting for the first time? So, then, we concluded that maybe this girl had had fifty to seventy meetings or something, and she just wasn't interested in chit-chatting. You know how you get so bitter and disillusioned when you keep meeting, and then it starts becoming a very mechanical thing.'

Or maybe there is something completely wrong about a system that expects people to make up their minds in a single meeting. Of course, a good meeting does not mean marriage, but a bad meeting does mean the marriage is off. The set-up doesn't make allowance for bad days and honesty.

'The sad part is that there are normal guys and girls out there, but they won't open up, because there are all these restrictions on what is considered eligible, and most won't dare break those. People cannot behave like people—a young man and a young girl can't have a stress-free, free-flowing conversation because you're constantly judging and gauging. In a real arranged set-up, that's how it is.'

The horoscope hurdle

As if all the restrictions weren't bad enough, there's also the question of horoscopes. While many people are open to their children having love marriages, an arranged marriage comes with all the traditional trappings, including horoscopes. It's hard enough to find a person whose photograph doesn't put one off. And within that, it's harder to find someone whom you know you may have dated if you'd been introduced under different circumstances. And when all this is right, there is yet another hurdle—horoscopes.

'I've known some people who say let's not even consider horoscopes, it's a big enough deal to find people who want to meet each other. That said, everyone is a little happier and feels more positively about things when horoscopes do match. I do, too. Maybe there is some science or logic to reading the stars, maybe it bodes well for the longevity of a relationship. But I wouldn't dismiss something just because it's not a match. Of course, there are lots of families who won't proceed unless the horoscopes match. And though it can be disappointing, and irritating, especially when you know it could work with that guy, you need to accept it. I tell myself I wouldn't be happy in a family that gives more importance to horoscopes than to whether a guy and a girl gel when they meet.'

But Devyani adds, 'It's annoying when someone wants a horoscope even to decide whether you should meet, but that we're also judging them in saying this, smacks of narrowmindedness. Maybe something has happened in the family, maybe one person believes in horoscopes, but they could turn out to be really nice, broadminded people. So, I think, you do what you must, and leave the rest up to God or fate or whatever you believe in.'

Horoscopes are sometimes asked for because they make for a more polite excuse than the truth—that someone is unattractive, or unable to make conversation, or in any other way undesirable. In this case, they're handy to have as a sort of insurance. But in this case, they're not particularly relevant as a hurdle, since they don't stand in the way of the couple having a meeting, albeit a disastrous one.

After some time, it is possible for the idea, that one may meet one's partner for life, to start fading.

However, Devyani is optimistic about the prospect of an arranged marriage, and says one shouldn't get into negative mode. 'It *can* happen that you meet the person the first time, and you feel so comfortable that you don't feel like it's the first time, and you don't feel like you're meeting him with the agenda of marriage. I've been told by friends of mine that it's happened to them. That there is chemistry, and you're clicking, and you know "this is it".'

Most people do believe in destiny, but one does need to be level-headed about things too. Having a panic attack can put paid to destiny. Devyani agrees. 'If you think a guy is nice, don't get bogged down by anything else. Try to forget the people breathing down your neck, and what meeting two or three times or whatever could mean. Just go for it. I do think what's meant to be will happen, and what's not meant to be won't happen. I don't know, since it hasn't happened to me yet, but I've been told that it all suddenly falls into place and clicks, it just happens. Maybe there's some sense to it, because everyone says the same thing.'

The wedding hungama

Brides tell us just how crazy a wedding day can get, why you're unlikely to remember it, and how to handle everything that goes wrong on the big day.

Chances are that you will not remember your wedding. It's the day you spend months planning for; it's the day that will be commemorated in photographs; it's the day that will yield your Facebook profile picture for your honeymoon-sanctioned absence from networking, and for several forthcoming anniversaries.

But, sadly, this is the day that very rarely lives up to the bride's fantasies, irrespective of how much work goes into making it perfect. Relatives, priests and Murphy's Law will ensure that it is a comedy of errors. Of course, this means it lends itself to oft-repeated stories for friends, family, children and grandchildren. First, though, a bride should learn to laugh at everything that goes wrong.

Take the case of Uttara Singh Chauhan. For all Uttara's expertise at organization, her wedding day turned out to be as insane and chaotic as that of any other bride.

She'd fixed an appointment at the salon for 4 p.m., so that she would reach the venue of the wedding by 6 p.m. The baraat was expected at 7 p.m., and of course, they're usually late, but she wasn't taking chances.

Her family had other ideas. Someone thought of another puja that hadn't been accommodated in the original schedule of rituals, and it was 5 p.m. before she left for the salon. At the salon, more than ten brides were having their make-up done—as they will be on every über-auspicious day—and one specialist was running around between them. He was throwing more tantrums than the brides, and a couple of them ended up crying, which made him furious, since he would have to do their make-up all over again.

Uttara quickly became his favourite because she laughed away and offered to do some of her make-up herself. She knew how it was done, thanks to her career in television anchoring. But the specialist spent more time on Uttara's make-up, at the cost of the other brides' schedules, and she was done by 6.45 p.m. She and her friends rushed off to the venue, and reached by 7.05 p.m. From outside, they saw the tail end of the baraat disappearing.

'They actually came on time!' she gasped, in disbelief. Now, they had to figure out a way for her to go in. She had more than twenty missed calls from her family. A friend of hers threw a dupatta over her, and they parked the car in a corner, switching off the headlights. Another friend made calls, and eight other friends, who were already at the venue, were asked to come to the car.

An advance party set out to keep watch. With a dupatta thrown over her bridal finery, and tall friends around her to keep her hidden, Uttara slowly—and nervously—sauntered into the venue, moving towards her room. Her brother and cousins had been asked to keep the groom's party occupied.

'Thank God for mobile phones. They saved the day,' she sighs.

In the case of Shreya Gopal and Rajiv Venkatesh, their wedding was a combination of Malayali and Tamil rituals. Since her family isn't religious or ritualistic or superstitious, they were completely clueless about what to do. To make it worse, the priest had to be changed at the last minute, since the first one came up with bizarre rituals that neither side saw the point in.

'I think the second guy may have been senile,' says Shreya. 'He suddenly decided we should have a Vedic ceremony, whatever that means. He made me sit on a chair, and my husband tied the thaali (mangalsutra) around my neck. And then he refused to allow the nadaswaram to be played. And he wouldn't let us play those games you usually do after the wedding, which are supposed to tell you who'll dominate the relationship or whatever. In the end, no one knew what was going on. So, finally, we gave up. If they asked us to stand, we stood; sit, we sat; wake up early in the morning, put oil in your hair and get doused with water, okay.'

She says some things need to be taken for granted, such as:
❖ Things are bound to go wrong on your wedding day

❖ Everyone organizes a grand wedding, and then wishes they'd chosen a temple ceremony instead

❖ Whatever you do, there will always be a family friend who orders about someone in the groom's family

❖ There will always be someone who gets offended and creates a scene

❖ There will be a last-minute demand for some sentimental ritual from one of the two families

But whatever a bride does, she shouldn't get involved with all this, Shreya says. 'This is for the adults. Let them have their arguments, let them panic, let them sort it out. For you and your fiancé to be involved in any way except to sit there and look nice is a mistake. We both woke up to it only after, and we were like hello, why did *we* get all agitated.'

In Shreya's case, her mother had fractured her arm. So most of the work was divided between Shreya and her aunt.

'The night before my wedding, my dad had a party for all his army friends, and I went there, came back home, and was packing my bag for the next day. The rest of my family was already at the hotel. My brother calls up, and says "Hey, I need to get my outfit for tomorrow. Can you keep it ready and put it on my bed?" So, the night before my wedding, I'm fishing out my brother's clothes, and ironing his kurta, and finding a new veshti and mundu and shoes and putting them all in his room. And then I walked out, and realized I'd forgotten the slippers I was going to wear, and had to rush back.'

Laughing, Shreya adds, 'But it gets worse. On my wedding day, my mother comes up to me and says, "So, umm, we need to pick up some things from home. What's kept where?" So much for the bride's right to throw tantrums.'

Smriti Rao's advice is to reconcile oneself early to the fact that one does not have much of a say in anything.

'I just felt like an actor being directed in a large production and I just played my part,' she says. 'Sometimes it felt like you're stepping outside your body and watching all the chaos around you. It's quite amusing!'

What do couples fight about in the first year?

It's often said that if a couple can get through the first year of marriage, they can weather any storm. And though Sara's and Sunil's first year was a bigger trial than most, with each having to deal with severe health problems, they also had their little battles throughout the grand war.

'The biggest problem? Oh, Sunil snores so loudly, and I'm such a light sleeper—it would get me so irritated! Then he got me ear plugs. It's not like they solved the problem, but they made it better, and I slowly got used to it. Sometimes, when I can't bear it, I go to the other room.'

Of course, they fight over who takes the garbage out.

But what really riles Sara is his tendency to leave wet towels on the bed. 'Ewww!' she shudders. 'Thank God, now he doesn't do it that often. But when I'm travelling on work, or I head off to visit family and friends, I still dread coming back to find the house in a mess.'

That's not to say there's nothing about her that doesn't make Sunil grind his teeth, quite literally. His big grouse is the way she handles the toothpaste. She tends to squeeze whichever part of the tube she touches first, whereas he is finicky about squeezing it out from the end.

To a newly married couple, no issue is too small to fight over—not even a tube of toothpaste.

Gayathri Mohan, however, testifies to the possibility of a harmonious relationship. She can't remember having any big fight in the first year. Her husband Sridhar is better at remembering anniversaries—down to that of their first meeting—than she is, so that was never an issue. But she says with fond frustration that going out together, especially on shopping expeditions, is practically a pipe dream. He would rather spend a quiet evening at home.

Shwetha Srinivasan says couples rarely fight over real problems in the first year. 'It's always external factors, it's about other people. Even now, that's what we usually fight about. And it's almost always me who initiates the fight. I must have done the yelling some 2000–3000 times. Only twice in our marriage has my husband shouted at me, and I got really scared. Well, I totally deserved both. But, yeah, fighting never happens because of *you*, it's always other things, and you need to see whether they're worth fighting over. Mostly, they're not.'

Smriti Rao and her husband Sagar got into tiffs in the first year of their marriage mostly because of miscommunication— they didn't understand what the other really meant.

'You're not sure whether the person is being romantic, cheeky, sarcastic, funny, or annoyed. It takes time to figure all that out, and to interpret facial expressions! And then, of course, there are those lifestyle values like whether you should buy a flashy car or a utility vehicle and so on. It's never important what you fight over, and you usually forget all of it, but how you handle it sets the tone for how you deal with things later.'

Past imperfect

Women tell us whether it makes sense to come clean about the past.

Vijaya Raghuraman feels disclosing one's past, and coming clean about boyfriends and relationships, depends entirely on who the spouse or spouse-to-be is, and how mature he is.

'It takes maturity to handle your partner's past. I told the first guy (with whom my engagement broke off) everything, and I also told Dileep everything. I feel it's better to be open, because then there is no room for suspicion. But then again, it depends on whom you're telling. If the other person doesn't want to know it, then it's best to just leave it. In my case, I did want to know about his past, but I also felt that if he didn't want to tell me, it was okay, it wasn't going to affect me. That's another thing you should look at. It's not about whether you want to know and you want to disclose your past alone—you need to take the other person's feelings into account. He has a right not to know, and he has a right not to tell. And so do you.'

Shreya Gopal is of the opinion that the past is best left behind. After their engagement, she and Rajiv discussed whether they wanted to make a full disclosure.

'He was like, "Look, you grew up in a city. I grew up in a city. We've both done city things. Plus, you're an army officer's daughter. So you've obviously grown up in a family that's okay with trusting you to handle your freedoms. You've had way more freedom than my sisters. I'm assuming you're allowed late nights and partying and drinking. And I know for a fact that the late nights are going to have to stop, because you're going to be with me in a cantonment. Unless I go to war, and you're back here, you're not going to be partying into the wee hours. And hopefully you won't do that when I'm at war."'

Shreya says it's very difficult to find someone who acknowledges that his wife's past is none of his business. 'Because people don't want to let go of your past—they want details of your relationship, what your boyfriends were like, how intimate your relationship was. But, with Rajiv, it was like, "I trust you to have enough integrity not to cheat on me. And, unless something happens in our marriage, our pasts are not each other's concern."'

Madhumitha Prasad's tip is to never talk to a spouse about an ex. 'I don't think anyone requires to know about his or her spouse's ex. Bringing up one's past life can only lead to disharmony in a marriage, and it is completely unnecessary,' she says.

Smriti Rao says making a decision about whether to make a full disclosure or not is one of the most difficult ones to handle.

'The later you get married, the harder it is to bring someone up to speed with what's been part of your life for all these years! With me, Sagar was very clear that he really didn't want to know anything, and he said it didn't matter to him. I think it sort of absolved me of judging myself, and then the fear of being judged. He's very mature in matters like this, and I think that's really cool. Of course, my first reaction was "Why does he not want to talk about the past, what do I need to know, what is he hiding from?" and so I shamelessly asked him!' she laughs. 'And he said I was more than welcome to ask, but there really was nothing worth telling.'

However, it *is* tricky territory to navigate, and Smriti says that starting on a clean slate should remain an axiom, especially in relatively late marriages.

The things our parents don't tell us

The ladies tell us about the things that can come as a surprise in a marriage.

While no one is short of unsolicited advice in the years, months, weeks, days, and even hours leading up to her wedding, not all of it comes in useful. And not everything that *could* be useful is said. There are some departments that brides are rarely told the right things about, but which turn out to be crucial aspects of a marriage.

Compromise

Most brides are sent off into marriages with the generic warning that life is all about compromise, or 'give-and-take'. However, no one really knows what compromise means, or what situations may arise in the first phase of a marriage.

Compromising on the wrong counts can quickly lead to

resentment, or to a shift in the balance of power that leaves one or both members of the couple unhappy.

Akhila Ravi feels compromise is acceptable when both people are doing it, 'even if the compromise is not totally fifty-fifty.'

And when is it not acceptable? 'If it goes against your individuality or if the compromise is forced on you by yourself or the other person, I'd say that will lead to resentment.'

'It is important to voice when you don't like the way something is playing out, and perhaps talk through a solution that doesn't hurt either person too much,' she says.

The epiphany

Shreya Gopal says the idea of marriage hits you some time into your relationship with your husband. 'The thing with marriage is that you're so caught up in the whole thing of oh, my God, I have saris to buy, things to do, friends to invite, I'm getting married in a few weeks, that you don't think, "Oh . . . wait, who is this man? I'm marrying him, and I don't know him from Adam." It doesn't occur to you at all. And then, when you're cooking, suddenly you have this epiphany—"I married a stranger." Don't panic. That's just how it is.'

Running a house

The switch from single woman to wife entails running a house, and this can often pose a huge challenge.

Living with family, there are several things we take for granted—that the bills will be paid, that the food will be on the table, that tea will be served. Living alone, or with roommates, we know that, worst-case scenario, we'll get by irrespective of what happens. A power cut usually means a midnight party on the terrace. When you run out of gas cylinders, you order in. When you've forgotten to buy provisions, you make do with chips and booze. But running your home mandates that you employ a servant and a cook, arrange a milkman and a newspaperboy, perhaps buy an inverter, keep tabs on the gas cylinder and make sure the electricity bill is paid. All this, while you continue to work.

In Sara Jacob's case, the shift wasn't quite drastic. She had already been living alone, and running a small place of her own, since she worked in Bangalore and her parents were based in Kuwait.

'Once I got married, what really changed was the fact that I had to remember to cook for another person,' she says. 'And also that the place we stayed in was not my house but *our* house. For that idea to settle down in both our heads took some time. In fact, in the first few months, Sunil would refer to our place as "your house". See, he's never stayed in a hostel or on his own, until he got married.'

And so he faced the tougher challenge. He was happy to be on his own, but most aspects of running a house were new and daunting. Initially, Sara had to take charge. It was she who saw to the bills being paid on time, it was she who got the newspaperboy to come in, and told him what he was to drop off. Eventually, though, Sunil took over most of the administration of their home.

Multi-tasking

'The multi-tasking is something you can't escape from,' Zainab Haider says. 'And every woman thinks "Oh, my God, how will I do it?!" And every woman manages to do it. It's there in our DNA—when we're pushed to those circumstances, into that situation, we are able to do it. And the funny thing is, you'll do it smoothly. It will come easily to you.'

She laughs when she thinks back to the early days of her own marriage. 'When I got married, I also thought, "Imagine, running a household, and thinking about aloo, pyaaz and dal, all these bills . . . I can barely take care of myself, I keep losing my mobile phone all the time, how am I going to coordinate all this?" Of course, initially, there will be teething problems. It's not like you'll run everything smoothly from Day One. But you do figure it out.'

Family matters

It is expected of a daughter-in-law to call up her husband's relatives and keep in touch with them, says Sara.

'Somehow, in Indian families, if the boy does not keep in touch with relatives or in-laws, it's fine, but *you're* expected to keep in touch with the guy's parents and his relatives. They say it's a woman's job, and I think it's high time that that changed.'

While a woman living with her parents doesn't usually have to call up her own relatives to enquire after their health when they take ill, or congratulate them on a wedding in the family, because her mother has already done that, things change after marriage. As a married woman, you aren't represented by your parents any more, and both your mother and you will have to make the courtesy calls.

However, this was routine for Sara. She hadn't stayed at home much since she finished school, and so she did make courtesy calls anyway, irrespective of whether her mother had or not.

In the kitchen

'How can I forget the biggie here . . . you *should* know how to cook. Write that down in capitals,' Sara laughs.

For all our concessions to the modern woman, she is still expected to run the kitchen. And when guests come home, they do expect a signature dish from the lady of the house, even if everything else is cooked by the help.

Fortunately for Sara, her parents had already told Sunil that she didn't know much about cooking. But, while he didn't expect culinary wonders from her, those visiting them at their new place did.

'They think you'll give them the sort of awesome meals your mother would have. It took me a proper year to make a decent meal for more than four!'

When to lie

Madhumitha Prasad feels modern marriage does entail some things that one has to figure out for oneself—things that our parents cannot, or will not, advise us to do.

'Like, lying sometimes to balance career, friends, family and interests,' she says. 'After a certain phase, you don't even have to tell your family all that you are doing outside home, like meeting friends after work or joining recreational classes of any kind. Take, for instance, when I was staying with my in-laws in Chennai and was working. By this time, I had a little daughter. Now, I used to go to dance classes on Saturdays, from 4 to 5 p.m. My mother-in-law would take care of my daughter on all the weekdays after she came back from school, and also for the few hours that I worked on Saturdays. I would finish work a little early and then go to dance classes. I didn't think it necessary to tell them that, lest they should feel that I was burdening them with childcare even on a Saturday, while I was dancing and having a nice time. On a bad day, even nice people—which my mother-in-law is—may tend to think that way, and I did not want that.'

Rules change

There are several generation-specific things parents don't tell us, Shwetha Srinivasan says, and that's because they can't. One of these is how to handle the pressure to have a baby. In our mothers' generation, a woman would be considered barren if she didn't have a child one year into her marriage. Timing a baby is one of the things very few parents can advise on.

'The other thing is that the rules in your in-laws' home will always be different from those in one's own,' says Shwetha. 'My mother herself wasn't brought up in as conservative a household as my in-laws' home. Some of the rules they had made me feel like I was in an old book. Like, I've never worn a nightie in my life. I find them very uncomfortable. I wear pyjamas at home. Now, both cover your legs properly. But to my in-laws, it was like, "Ooooh, she's sitting around in pyjamas, it's so untraditional!" and I'm like, how does it matter? Unless I'm sitting in nine yards, nothing is traditional, no?'

But there is one piece of advice her mother gave her, which has stood her in good stead. And that was to talk to her husband, and make him a friend and ally. 'She said, even if he's a quiet chap—which my husband is—you need to keep talking to him, tell him everything, become friends. And she's taught me well. That's really helped.'

Your husband is not your girlfriend

A husband may be a good friend, but he's not going to be a girlfriend—he may not even be a boyfriend. One of the things women are caught unawares by is that their need for validation is often unfulfilled, Zainab Haider points out. Husbands don't dish out compliments like mothers and roommates and gal pals do. You're not told you're a superwoman for doing up your place, taking care of your children, working out and doing well at your job. And the certainty that comes with marriage appears to make husbands less passionate—and less eager-to-please—than boyfriends are. Over time, the romantic flourishes and the birthday surprises tone themselves down.

'It doesn't mean you're not appreciated,' Zainab says. 'I think men just aren't built to say the things that women do. They're quick to point out mistakes, but you have to worm every little compliment out of them!' Perhaps that's why it's important for a woman to maintain her own circle of friends, and have a life outside the marriage too. Often, couples befriend couples. Even more often, the wives of one's husband's friends become one's friends. This isn't enough. Your friends from school, college and work, who've seen you in different roles, who themselves are in different stages of a relationship, can provide you with a support system.

'How do I jump into bed with someone I don't know?'

So, we don't do the chai-tray, bride-examination-ceremony any more. So, we meet grooms, and get to know them, and establish that they're not serial killers. But, we can't escape the fact that in a relationship it is often physical attraction that brings a couple together, whereas this is not so in an arranged marriage. While most couples brought together by horoscopes and family sneak a kiss or two, maybe even a cuddle, premarital sex is out of the question. Sometimes, the question of having to share a bed with a man who has been gauged by all other practical concerns is neatly brushed under the carpet.

But one fine day, you're married, and you know you're supposed to be having sex. Everyone wants you to make babies, but no one has spoken about chemistry. How does one undress in front of a man one barely knows?

Swatilekha Mukherjee found herself dealing with this problem. More than two weeks into her marriage, she wasn't able to bring herself to sleep with her husband. He was uncomfortable too, and they would give up at some point within the first few days. After that, they simply went to bed without broaching the subject, or making any moves towards each other. Neither was comfortable discussing it with friends or family, and Swatilekha began to look up internet forums, to see whether anyone had spoken about this.

'It's amazing how many people have this problem. They're all worried about whether they will ever find chemistry, or ever be comfortable enough to have sex. Isn't it supposed to happen naturally? Clearly, it's something the previous generation hasn't thought much about. Most of us assume our parents had a celibate relationship—I mean, most of them don't even hold hands in public— but we're all here, so clearly they didn't. But many women in this generation, even women who have slept with boyfriends earlier, find it difficult to get this aspect of their lives going.'

She found the advice from users on the forum ranged from discussing the subject and taking it slow, to watching porn, heading to a cold vacation spot, trying hypnosis, giving role-play a shot, and getting drunk.

'Someone suggested reading Ghalib's shayaris out to each other. There was even a mini-*Kamasutra* in there, with advice on how best to titillate your partner and yourself, when you're not very comfortable. Down to using soft voices.' Eventually, someone said 'Blue film is against Indian culture', and of course, the rest of the thread was an argument.

However, Swatilekha did find some handy advice—physical comfort evolves from emotional comfort. 'If you aren't able to sleep together, don't worry. First, get to know each other properly. In the first few days of marriage, you aren't even able to confide in each other about things like problems with the family, or trouble at the workplace. How are you going to sleep together at that stage? Of course, if you've had a long courtship and have spent time getting to know each other, it may be different. But if you haven't, you should relax and take it slow.'

She discussed it with her husband, and they decided there was no hurry. They finally did sleep together, but it happened nearly five months into their marriage.

Brinda Sundar feels part of the problem is that our idea of sex is different from the actual act, which makes everyone's first experience something of a shock. 'The problem is that women, especially if they're virgins—like I was—have big expectations from sex. We grow up thinking it's going to be like something, and then you feel all embarrassed and dirty when it actually begins to happen. I turned to an older friend for advice, and she told me not to overthink it. First, we need to understand that marriage is not *Mills and Boon*. It's not even *Sex and the City*.'

And then, there are those couples for whom sex will always be perfunctory. They may have had relationships with others in which the chemistry was great. They themselves may be attractive people. But sometimes, it simply doesn't click. However, this isn't a good enough reason to call off a marriage.

'I think it's important for there to be some amount of intimacy,' Brinda says. 'You don't know how the sex is going to be, of course, in an arranged marriage, but you can gauge whether you're comfortable with someone. *That* is the foundation of a marriage, not the act itself. You're not a teenager, your libido isn't the most important thing in the world.'

Valerie D'Souza had a long relationship with her boyfriend, but chose to have an arranged marriage when the relationship ended. She had had a sexual relationship with her boyfriend, and doesn't find as much chemistry with her husband. 'I've learnt to accept it, though. Sex isn't everything, there's more to a marriage. There *are* times when I think back to how it used to be with my boyfriend, but then I also remember that I am much more secure and happy in the marriage. Also, the fact that your sex life isn't great does not mean you may be tempted to sleep around. I don't know how to explain it, but there's a certain bond in just the act of the ring going over your finger. And I've always stayed faithful to my husband.'

Of course, a celibate marriage doesn't work, but a marriage where the couple isn't constantly hungering for each other's bodies *can* work, as long as they're not repulsed by each other.

The many guises of dowry

Brides and their families speak about the new trend of men asking for a 'working woman'.

Dowry has always been a delicate subject. There are those who justify its entry into the Indian marriage system—it was a means of ensuring the financial security of a bride, at a time when women did not go out to work, had no source of income, and didn't stand to inherit their parents' property.

Of course, it became a money-making venture, and still is. However, the issue of dowry harassment is seen as something that people who belong to a less privileged socio-economic class must deal with.

Even so, there are subtler ways of making money from a bride. And this may be one of the reasons for the new mandate that women should work after marriage. The 'homely' in matrimonial advertisements has given way to 'educated' and 'working woman'.

As the grandfather of a friend put it, 'Earlier, they wanted a one-time dowry; now they want it every month.'

'The funny thing is, the previous generation's main concern was whether they would be allowed to work after marriage. In ours, I think the main concern is whether we will be able to quit after marriage,' says Vidya Gaekwad. 'It's not like I intend to be a housewife, but I think my career is my own business. We were once approached by a family that said they're particular about a working woman for a daughter-in-law. Not only that, they wanted a specific salary bracket. I was so tempted to ask whether their son intended to be a homemaker after marriage. I think I raised my eyebrows or something, and his mother quickly told me, "You know, an educated woman shouldn't be wasting her education. And nowadays, in Mumbai, if you want a good flat, it's all so expensive. How will one person alone work?" And then, she gave me some more gyan. It boiled down to roti will be taken care of, but if you want a nice kapda and nice makaan, you have to earn it.'

Sometimes, it becomes an excuse for families to show off their wealth. There are those who choose to have simple weddings, and invest the money they would have splurged on a grand wedding in something for the newly-weds. In some cases, it's as pragmatic as a fixed deposit; in some cases, it's furniture.

There is a general belief that it is unbecoming of a bride's family to send their daughter to a new home 'empty-handed'. But feminists may take heart from the fact that this sentiment is no longer restricted to the girl's side alone.

Ruchika Solanki says her wedding became a contest between

the two families. 'One sponsored our honeymoon, the other bought us furniture, one redid the flat, the other stocked our kitchen, one bought us a car, the other bought us a bigger car. So, I think nowadays dowry is a show-off thing, and honestly, that makes the couple's lives very easy.'

However, there are traditional demands for dowry too, and modern families have their own ways of tackling them.

Radhika Nair says, 'Among Mallus, it's still a done thing. Some people even come up with lists: "Oh, we need 200 sovereigns, and of course, she has her own car?" Or, "The girl has a diamond necklace, right?" In one case, the boy had studied in Australia and was working there, and these people wanted us to, like, tell them what sort of jewellery is available. *Available.* My father very politely said, "What jewellery is available? Like, gold specifically? See, there's the door, get out, go down the stairs, take an auto to T. Nagar, and you can ask the salesmen what's available, and buy it. Thanks, and have a nice day."'

You marry the man, not the family

We speak about why women can be tempted to marry a man because his family is so wonderful. But sadly, the cooler the family is, the more time you're going to have to spend alone with the man who doesn't match up.

'Why is it that the attractiveness of a man is inversely proportional to the attractiveness of his mother?' Devyani Khanna sighs.

She doesn't mean physical attractiveness alone. Often, it happens that a man's family has far more going for it than he has going for himself. It can happen that one connects better with the family than the prospective husband. When that happens, the urge to marry into a family that is so perfect and makes one so comfortable can override the awareness that the man is not the best match.

Part of the reason is that the nicer the in-laws are, the more non-interfering they are. And therefore, they will give their daughter-in-law enough time and space for her to discover that she married the wrong man, for the wrong reasons.

I myself have often been swayed by this temptation. Every time a woman I knew asked me for my mother's number, I knew why. And though I was always somewhat resistant to the idea of arranged marriage, my curiosity would get the better of me, at least in my early twenties. At the time, my big condition was that a man should be funny enough to be able to stop a fight by making me laugh.

The problem, I would discover, is that everyone assumes his or her son, or grandson, or nephew, or brother, is funny. I would also discover that the funny bone in the family is not inherited by all its members.

One of the prospective mothers-in-law I spoke to was so much fun, and so easy to get along with, that I wanted to marry her son just so I could hang out with her. Her son had neither her charm nor her wit. Thankfully, most people have blogs, and it's hard to ignore the writing on the wall. However, I did manage to stay in denial for a few weeks.

I told myself there would always be some compromise involved, and that relationships do involve compromise too. There was no reason not to marry him. His mother was awesome, his family seemed fun, and he was well-mannered. But the lack of reasons not to marry someone isn't good enough reason to marry him.

Sitting at a table one night with friends who had come in from out of town, I realized that I could relate to each of the men smoking and joking around me better than I could to the man I was considering marriage with. Every single one of them was funnier, more intelligent and better suited to a life with me. Now, I understood why I would feel a sinking low every time he called. I had fooled myself into thinking it was because I'm not much of a talker, but I have spoken to friends on the phone for hours, and I had to confront the fact that this prospect should not go further.

There are times when a family is more enthusiastic about marriage than a man is, and a friend of mine had this experience. She was drawn to him because he seemed sophisticated. He didn't interview her, as it were. He didn't want to know her hobbies, and they spoke about random things, without mentioning marriage. But, after a point, when she had to bring it up, he began to stammer. It hit her that he wasn't quite sure about what he wanted; he was probably being pressurized into marriage. There was no point persisting with it. When she asked him outright, he denied it, but it didn't feel right.

One of the reasons Vijaya Raghuraman decided to get engaged to the man things eventually broke off with was that she got along with his family so well. It became apparent that she and he were not cut from the same cloth, but it was only something as drastic as his dating someone else on the sly that prompted her to break off the engagement.

Now, there may also be a case where a man makes up for his family. In Shwetha Srinivasan's case, her husband helped her deal with demanding in-laws. He was supportive of her decisions, understanding of her need to put her foot down and willing to mediate when things threatened to get ugly.

Women who have grown up in big cities, and had exposure to bigger ones, tend to look for cosmopolitan families. But that's irrelevant if one is going to live in a small town. One of the men I was put in touch with had a job that would necessarily keep him in small, industrial towns. The only cities I've lived in are Chennai, Delhi and London, each larger than the previous one. It struck me that I couldn't fathom life where I wouldn't find at least one classy twenty-four-hour restaurant, where book launches wouldn't happen, where authors wouldn't make a compulsory stopover on a multi-city tour, where streets weren't busy till at least 11 p.m., which didn't have an eating joint that would deliver at midnight, where I didn't have reason to crib about Metro construction, where someone I knew wouldn't have a 'guy' for everything that needed bootlegging.

One may pride oneself on pragmatism and say 'certain compromises' must be made. But the pragmatism needs to go beyond the family, and sometimes, beyond the man.

Rejection; inflicting it, handling it

Women speak about the danger of succumbing to pressure from relatives, and also the other side—how to handle rejection from the groom's family.

One of the most delicate aspects of handling an alliance is learning how to reject it. One just may end up succumbing to pressure to avoid hurting one's relationships with the family friends or relatives who vouch for the boy.

Shreya Gopal feels it's important to make the family understand that this is *your* choice, since you're the one who's going to be living the life they've conjured up for you. 'This is not like a job that you can quit after three or, maximum, five years. This is a twenty-five, thirty, thirty-five, forty-year investment that you're making. That's not something you can take lightly. You need to like the person you're marrying, you need to be able to talk to him, that's the minimum requirement—the other things you may compromise on, like his skin colour, or the job he's doing, but you have to at least like the guy. If you can't talk to him for even an hour, what are you going to do with the rest of your life? And it *will* take you some time to find this partner, especially if you've grown up in a city, and been given a good education, and have had the sort of independence I have. Your husband needs to be someone you can relate to, intellectually, mentally, emotionally.'

Shreya has a good relationship with most of the older generation of her family, and her relatives are broadminded enough to understand her choices and reservations. So, though Shreya did turn down some men her relatives were keen for her to marry, that didn't have any impact on the cordiality of her relationship with the aunts and uncles concerned.

While rejecting a man gracefully is hard enough, it's even tougher to have to deal with being rejected. But one does need to be prepared to take it in one's stride, and learn not to let it affect one's self-confidence. There could be several extraneous factors that lead a man to reject a woman—he may already have a girlfriend, whom the family is unwilling to accept; it's possible that the horoscopes really don't match, and it isn't simply an excuse; it may be as ridiculous as someone tripping over a threshold while leaving the girl's house.

But the instinctive reaction to rejection is for one to feel miserable, and wonder what is wrong with oneself—isn't it?

'No,' says Devyani Khanna, 'When things don't work out, they usually mutually don't work out. You can figure out in the meeting itself. And there's also the question of pressure. If I'm more eager to get married—because of family, or age, or whatever—I may say yes even if my heart is not in it. Whereas if the boy is not in as much a hurry, he may not say yes unless he really likes me. So, you may react differently to it, but you *do* know whether you have chemistry.'

Even if the attraction—or repulsion—is one-sided, it's important not be deflated by it. Devyani recalls an instance where she met a man whom there was nothing wrong with, but whom she didn't like because she found him too staid and serious. 'I would prefer someone who's light-hearted, whom I can laugh with. But this guy didn't seem to have much of a sense of humour. He was talking seriously all through. I didn't see it working. And then, there are times when the parents are more enthusiastic about the marriage than the guy. He may call you once in two weeks, but they call every other day and ask you what your inclination is. There's no point pursuing something like that. Rejection doesn't mean there's something *wrong* with someone, it just means you don't get along. When one person has misgivings, chances are that both do. Maybe it has potential, but it isn't working.'

Smriti Rao says she never felt the pinch of a match falling through, because she didn't feel she had much at stake. The mindset with which she had got into the arranged marriage circuit was so casual that it was almost experimental.

'Sometimes, it's fun to see what excuses people come up with,' Smriti says. 'Mostly, it's that the horoscopes don't match. Or, you suddenly decide you're not ready for marriage. I've only been turned down once, and they said they wanted an engineer bride.'

However, no one likes to be rejected, either on a pretext, or for a valid reason, and it does need preparation.

'It does worry you, and you start wondering whether

the grounds are real,' she says, 'But I'd say try not to think too much about it. Just go in with a let's-see-what-comes-of-it attitude.'

Your space, my space

We look at the trust factor—sharing passwords, sharing details of bank accounts. Is this always a good idea? Should one make a conscious effort at this?

Sharing passwords is a tricky thing. Everyone has different attitudes to privacy, and partners in an arranged marriage are not always soulmates. And, often, they don't know each other well enough to refuse a request. This can lead to resentment later, or, as Preethi Madhavan would find out, worse.

Almost as hard to approach is the subject of salaries. The days of the 'biodata' or 'CV' are over. People hesitate to ask each other about salaries. No one wants to be seen as the sort of person who would marry for money. At the same time, finances come into play almost as soon as a couple is married—should they rent or buy a home? Where should they live? What sort of accommodation can they afford? How about gifts for birthdays? Where do they celebrate? Can they go on holiday?

'Very honestly, I never even asked Dileep how much he

used to earn. To me, it didn't matter, because I knew that if there was any problem, he was going to tell me,' Vijaya Raghuraman says. 'As soon as we were married, he told me his salary. As for passwords, it all happened automatically. He travels a lot, and sometimes he can't access his email and needs something done, so he asks me to do it for him. The same thing goes for credit card numbers and passwords. We know each other's Netbanking passwords, we do transactions on each other's behalf. He's into investment advisory, so he does my investments. I hate sorting money out, and he loves it, so that solves the problem for me!'

She feels the idea of a joint account is outdated. 'We haven't felt the need for one. It's not like in our parents' times, when a joint account helped you handle money when the other person was not around. With technology, you can access anything from anywhere. Also, at the time, even having one account was a big deal. But now, people have so many accounts in so many banks and branches that it sometimes becomes difficult to keep track of all of them!'

They don't feel that having email passwords is an invasion of space or privacy. With a laugh, Vijaya Raghuraman says she does chat about Dileep, though only with close friends. 'It's not like he's going to check my chats, but even if he does, it's okay. He knows what I think about him anyway, and I know what he thinks about me.'

Meera Anthony feels one doesn't need to have The Talk about money in a hurry. Living together doesn't really mean one has to sit down and budget everything, even small spends.

'We discussed finances for the first time when we were

thinking about buying a house a year and a half ago,' Meera says. That was a year and a half into their marriage. They did have access to each other's accounts, and transparency in their spending, but they hadn't spoken about salary. She doesn't remember when exactly they exchanged Netbanking details. She feels it's best to let it happen naturally, rather than allow for an awkward moment in the first months of marriage.

However, in some cases, the question of finances becomes crucial such as when a woman has to give up her career, or take a break, and suddenly loses her financial independence. This was the case with Shreya Gopal, who had to move into an army cantonment right after marriage.

One of the things she liked most about Rajiv was that, though he respected her privacy and her need for space, he was clear that there would be no 'yours' and 'mine'—it would be 'we'. He recognized that to be with him Shreya would have to quit her job and possibly switch to a less lucrative freelancing option.

'So, he said, "There's no 'my money' and 'my flat'. If you're giving up work to be with me, I know it's going to be something you'll have to live with every day, and I don't want you feeling that you're living off me. These are combined resources, and this is money you'd have had if you were working, so chill." For me to find someone who thinks like that is a big deal. And it was not just in theory, I can see every day that he's held good on it. He told me this is my show, and I may please run it how I want to—the house, our finances, everything.'

Living with in-laws: does it make sense?

What are the advantages and disadvantages of living with in-laws? Most brides seem to think there are close to no advantages; or, at least, that the trade-off is not worth it.

One of the early challenges a couple has to deal with is waking up to how a house is run. Does this, perhaps, put more pressure on people who are already on edge? One has to go to work, get used to being around a new presence and keep house. When couples live in the same city as their in-laws, does it make sense to move in with them for a few months?

Sara Jacob doesn't think so. She didn't do it, and she wouldn't recommend it.

'For one thing, you're getting used to someone living with you 24×7. It takes a lot of adjusting and when you're getting used to the whole idea of being married, the last thing you want is having to deal with a new set of people.'

She feels staying with in-laws will not only hamper a couple's independence, but will also cut into the time they get to spend with each other. It's the easy way out, for those who leave the burden of running the house to the in-laws. Sara isn't comfortable with the idea that a married person has no clue about how to run a house. And anyway, the lack of responsibility isn't worth the lack of freedom living with the in-laws entails.

'It also depends on what kind of in-laws you have,' Sara says, and points out that one shouldn't have to walk on eggshells in one's home.

Smriti Rao feels being alone together, and away from either's in-laws, helped her and Sagar get to know each other.

'The two of us were left to work things out, and that's the best,' she says, 'because, I think a lot of stereotypes are driven by society, and reinforced by family, and they can influence your expectations of one another. When you're just two of you, those expectations don't play out as much.'

Another factor that helped was that both of them had worked in other cities, and were used to living with roommates. 'I think we were actually like roomies to begin with,' she laughs. 'And that takes a lot of the pressure off.'

According to Shwetha Srinivasan, it's very important to live away from in-laws in an arranged marriage set-up, because that's when one really gets to know one's husband.

'What I am in front of my parents is really what I am. That's how I am with you, with my husband, in office, with other people. But my husband—and maybe it's true of most men—is a totally different person with his parents from what he is with me, with friends, even with my family! He can be incredibly jolly, but he gets quiet when his parents are around. It's taken him eight years to even talk to me in front of them, to call me by name. Earlier, he'd just start off with, "You know what . . .", and I was supposed to understand that it's meant for me. It was a very slow, but steady, transition. It wouldn't have happened if we'd stayed with the in-laws.'

She points out there are other problems too. A couple doesn't get its own space, and there will always be a clash with the older generation. 'It's quite normal, in our age group, to decide to eat out on impulse. If we're out, sometimes we have dinner, and say oh, we'll keep whatever's at home for breakfast tomorrow. But with in-laws, you won't have that freedom. They don't get the concept of re-heating. They'll go on about wasting food, wasting money. And if they interfere in these tiny things, it gets difficult. That's why I respect my mother-in-law for saying you take care of your family, I'll take care of mine. Even if she doesn't help now with the baby, that's fine—because we have other ways to see that the baby is well looked after. But if they'd messed with us every day, it would have been super-difficult. I would say, stay separately at least for some time, and once you both understand each other fully, then you can think about getting into this whole *Hum Aapke Hain Kaun* set-up.'

'The clock is ticking'

Is there a right age for marriage?

One of the biggest dilemmas women face is when to get married. Do you complete your studies and get married? Do you wait till you have some perspective on life? Do you do all of this in parallel? On the one hand, getting married early could help you grow *with* your husband, rather than have to search for a husband who fits in with the rigid views of a 30−32-year-old you. On the other hand, do you know who you really are when you're in your early twenties? Should you be making a decision that will affect the next half-century of your life?

When you're a girl, and of a certain age, and your friends are getting married all around you, you may think the people constantly telling you that marriage is all about compromise, and that no marriage is perfect, are right. You may worry that the pool of eligible men is getting smaller. Mothers tell their daughters it would be a good idea to have children when the grandmothers are still young enough to help. Besides, women are told, the last thing you want to do in your thirties is chase a hyperactive kid around the house.

But the need to know oneself is not simply existential angst. It has ramifications on a relationship. What if you grow up, find out the person you married is not the sort of person you can live with, and grow resentful of him, your parents and even yourself? What if the marriage turns ugly, and you can't walk out because you don't want to put your children through a divorce?

Though there are no real certainties, chances are that a woman in her late twenties or early thirties knows at least what she is willing to compromise on, and what she is not.

Ruhani Kapoor did get married early, but she stops short of recommending any particular course of action. 'The older I get, the more grey areas I see in life. I don't think there is one right answer. There are pros and cons to both early and late marriage. Everyone is different, and so are his or her requirements and preferences.'

There *are* advantages to getting married early—you grow up together with your spouse, and figure each other out along the way. However, Ruhani says, there are no guarantees that two people will evolve the same way. 'A fellow poet and close friend, who recently got divorced, met her husband when she was in college. She realized that while she had learnt to become his wife along with being a friend and a professional, he saw their marriage from the eyes of a twenty-year-old. But that said, when you get married early, there is a sense of security in the relationship—you don't need to mark your territory, so to speak, and deal with the insecurities stemming from a new relationship in the prime of your life: your thirties.'

She acknowledges the other side too. While someone in the thirties may come across as rigid, s/he would know what s/he wants as opposed to a 22-year-old, who may end up spending the twenties appeasing others, and then figuring out what s/he wants in the thirties. 'And, *bam*, they become this person that even they themselves might have a hard time recognizing. To quote a friend, "I think the 30s may be when self-awareness finally overturns the guilt of society and you start changing who you are to better suit your desires and not *theirs*." So, I do feel the thirties is when people blossom in many ways. It all evens out in the end, I guess.'

In Shreya Gopal's family, the women had always married relatively late. Some didn't marry at all. 'They're beautiful, intelligent, well-educated women, but they stayed unmarried either because they didn't find anyone they were compatible with, or because they simply didn't feel the need to get married.'

However, Shreya *was* sure she wanted to be married, at some point of time. Age was no cause for concern in her family, and her mother and aunts were unequivocal about one thing—she should never agree to an alliance for any reason other than that she liked the groom.

'I think the older you are, the better equipped you are to decide what sort of partner you want. You've had some kind of life experience, you've made some kind of money, you've made some sort of decision about the career you're interested in, and by then, you've learnt to stand up for what you want. There are certain things that you will negotiate, certain things that you absolutely will not negotiate. There are certain things that you're sure are a deal-breaker for you. This is a forty-year investment you're making, so you need to walk in with your set of terms and conditions.'

Shreya feels it's only in their late twenties that women know what these conditions are, and this is crucial. 'Because, otherwise, you'll get married to someone, and then you'll realize at some point that you've given in, given in, given in, given in, and you wake up a few years later and think, "Fuck, I don't want to do this any more!" and that's not cool. You need to be sure of what you want, and it's okay to ask for it. You've fought with your family for the right to wear sleeveless kurtas, the right to go out late at night, the right to drink, so I don't understand why you can't fight for the things you stand for, and the things you won't stand for, with a complete stranger, with whom you intend to spend the rest of your life.'

Gayathri Mohan got married when she was 24 years old. But, to her, it's not so much about age as about one's state of mind and one's place in life. 'The most important thing is that you need to be settled. You need to have some idea of what you want from life, you need to have chosen a career, and to have been able to handle yourself independently, I think. In my case, I was working, and I'd been living in a hostel, away from family. I was ready, in my own head. You can succumb to pressure from your parents, or relatives who are afraid they may not live to see you married. I had met two or three people before Sridhar, but I wasn't fully ready. I just wanted to get it over with.'

She's not sure age plays a major role in helping one make a

decision. Her nod to Sridhar was instinctive. 'I thought at the time that we would get along really well. In his case, I think he'd already made up his mind that he'd had enough of the bride hunt and would marry this girl irrespective of what she was like, you know. He gave me flowers on our first meeting. He claims he didn't give any of the other girls flowers!'

Though Shwetha Srinivasan herself was married at 22, she says there is no set formula. 'Some of my good friends got married at 21 (gasp!)—some of it worked, some didn't. Any marriage is a huge risk. It's not just about two people coming together, there are two families involved. Each of the stakeholders is pulling in all directions. At the end of the day, the husband and wife need to firmly believe they are meant to be together and shut out all the other environmental factors.'

She doesn't feel people get more set in their ways with age, either. 'Your personality keeps changing, you evolve with every external stimulus. That can vary from having a baby and getting into a new job, to retiring, or meeting with an accident—there are so many things an individual faces outside the marriage. Your partner needs to understand the changing dynamics, and somehow get along, and adjust and evolve with you. And you need to hold on to the belief that your spouse loves you. God, I feel like Oprah, so I'll stop.'

While Aarthi Varanasi acknowledges that marrying early and having both her children by the age of 27 has given her advantages, in retrospect, she still doesn't think one should get married in a hurry.

'Granted, now, at 38, I can take up a full-time job, go for late recordings and voiceover projects, do whatever I want, because my children are grown up. When I get a sudden call—because that can often happen in the industry—I can just go without having to worry about feeding them dinner, or giving them lunch. But 23 is not at all the right age to get married. It's too young to start a family. Marriage is a big commitment—a commitment to someone *and* his family—and a big responsibility.'

When one sees friends of one's own age either studying further, or making lots of money at cushy jobs, it can get one down, she says.

'In my case, the peer pressure made me think about whether getting married early and taking on all that responsibility was a mistake,' she says, 'That's when I decided I had to go back to work. I didn't want to make another mistake, otherwise I'd end up sulking and cribbing all my life. It's all bullshit when people say it helps you settle in early. Luckily, I have a supportive husband and understanding children. And the right opportunities came my way. But it doesn't happen for everyone. When you're starting off, you may not get a job with timings that suit your family. Nowadays, you need a solid education, you need a good job, something for your own security. Getting married at 25–26 is absolutely fine, but not earlier.'

Smriti Rao, too, was told an early marriage would be easier to settle into. Many of her cousins had married early, and their children were grown-up by the time they were in their thirties.

'But in my early and mid-twenties, I was more clueless than I was even in my teens. I was changing cities, changing jobs, trying to find a foothold. And when you're that confused, I don't think early marriage can work,' she says, 'But the best part of all this is that there is no one formula. It's different for different people, and there are pros and cons to both sides.'

It all boils down to one's personality, and how one sees oneself. Some people grow increasingly rigid, and are less likely to be able to accommodate a partner. On the other hand, there are those who enter a marriage in a hurry, get 'baby-ed' by their husbands and never learn to make their own decisions.

'For me, it would have been a disaster. I think you know when you're actually ready for marriage, and you need to go with that irrespective of what people tell you,' says Smriti.

The question of children

*Women speak about timing a baby, keeping relatives at bay,
how a baby alters the relationship, and how one handles the
news that one cannot have children.*

We may not belong to a generation that has to produce at least one child before the first wedding anniversary, just to show the world that both reproductive systems are in working order. But that doesn't mean the pressure has eased off, especially from older relatives.

Shwetha Srinivasan says, 'The harassment over having babies starts the minute the third knot is tied.' At 22, she was nowhere near ready to have a baby. Nor was it simply about her.

'It's not just the woman, it's the *couple* that needs to be ready to have a baby. Both the parents need to be able to spend enough time, money, effort in bringing up the baby. Well, it is also when the extended family—parents and in-laws—are ready too. Making a baby is team work—okay, you pervert, let me rephrase that . . . bringing up a baby is a team effort!'

Speaking from experience, Shwetha says it takes about a year for new parents to figure out how to put a howling baby to sleep. Until then, the support system provided by grandparents is critical.

She had a baby after five years of marriage, to the horror of most of her family; but she stayed firm that she wanted to finish most of her MBA without a toddler on her hands.

'Keeping the relatives at bay wasn't a big deal. No one can force you to do it, no? Of course, they won't understand your real reasons, or they'll have some contra-logic, so you use tactics. I tackled mine using multiple tools—anger, humour, changing the topic to a newly acquired diamond necklace, or scandalizing them. I remember, once I was on the phone with this really old, but close, relative of mine. She asked me about babies, and I told her we were actually thinking of making one right now, but she was holding us up from "you know what". That was the last time I heard her advice!'

Shwetha says, ideally, one should figure out what one wants to study, explore new job opportunities and plan well before settling down to start a family.

'Once you have a baby . . . well, let's just say, you don't have time to pee in peace. Literally. Someone else—mother, husband, whoever has agreed to babysit—needs to do you a favour before you can go to the bathroom. If this is the case to *pee,* you can understand the studying part. I used to get a couple of hours to study and, believe me, I made the most out of it.'

Gayathri Mohan sets a timeline, and says one must wait for two or three years into a marriage, rather than have a baby immediately. 'You need some time to settle down and enjoy your life. If you're working, that's also a factor. You *will* have to take a break, maybe a long one, for a baby. Again, just as with marriage, I would say don't succumb to pressure. Parents simply don't understand. Their generation didn't work like this. My mother and grandmother started pressurizing me within a year of marriage. And my relatives started asking about "good news" too. The thing is, only you will know when you're ready to have a baby.'

Having a baby doesn't necessarily alter the relationship in any way, Gayathri feels. 'I suppose there's a bond in the sense that we've made this child together, but I don't really sense much of a difference.' She pauses, and laughs, 'Except that, to Sridhar, I don't exist anymore. And our little boy is the spitting image of me, but Sridhar brings out his own baby photographs, and tries to prove that he takes after him. That's pretty hilarious.'

Dealing with the pressure to have children when one doesn't want to is pretty much a rite of passage. But what if a woman has trouble conceiving? What if a couple is told that they will not have children?

One of the main differences between a love marriage and an arranged marriage is that, in the first case, you know the person and love him for who he is. You didn't pick and choose him using the checkbox theory, at least not consciously. Something about him appealed to you. You liked certain things about him, and you liked him despite other things. And there was that determining factor that made you fall in love with him. You have a bank of memories, of stages in your romance, and you know you want to be with him, irrespective of what happens.

But, in an arranged marriage, you chose your partner for certain reasons—you wanted to settle down, you wanted to live in a certain city, you wanted to share your life with someone, you wanted to be married before you hit a particular age, you wanted children. Sometimes, you assume an arranged marriage will get you a made-to-order spouse to make your made-to-order life, complete with children. What happens if you can't have them?

Ruchika Solanki says the thought never occurred to her or Rohan. They fretted that they would have a baby before they were ready, not that they wouldn't be able to when they wanted to start a family. They didn't even discuss it.

But, she began to worry when a family scandal broke—a distant relative hadn't had children for four years after marriage. 'Everyone would ask him why, and they would treat his wife like she was a mutant,' she says. 'Later, we got to know the problem was some stress-related low sperm count. It was easily treatable, but, my God, the poor man was treated like a leper. Fortunately, he had a son, so his reputation has now been redeemed! Anyway, I decided I wasn't going to attract attention by leaving it too late. So, two years into our marriage, we started trying, and well, we didn't have to try too hard.'

They now have a son.

While Zainab Haider was speaking to me about her marriage, her daughter came running up to show her a drawing she had been working on. 'Oh, wow, you did this all by yourself?' Zainab exclaimed. 'It's very nice. Now, colour it and show it to me, okay?' As the little girl ran off, Zainab laughed about how, as a parent, one needs to be all enthusiastic and encouraging, *all the time*. 'These are the small joys of life that you have to cherish. What you say or think means so much to them.'

'You said you could imagine Haider being the father of your children,' I said, remembering an earlier point she had made, 'and that having children was important to you. Did you ever think about what would have happened if you hadn't been able to have them? You enter a marriage expecting it to give you everything you want.'

'Yes. And I've been lucky.' Zainab paused and thought. 'You know, we do know several couples who don't have children. And when I look at them, far from being bitter about it, or wishing they had married someone else, these couples are even closer to each other, I think, because it's just the two of them. Of course, everyone who can't have kids goes through a period of having medical tests and visiting fertility clinics and all that. But I think they eventually reconcile themselves to the fact.'

There are those who consider adoption. There are those who throw themselves into their careers. And there are those who take advantage of the fact that they don't have to time their vacations around summer holidays, and take off to exotic places and make all their friends envious. 'We're so tied down, you know, those of us with kids,' Zainab said. 'I feel they're compensated in other ways.'

There are others who put a positive spin on not being able to have children of their own. 'I have a friend who's running an NGO, and she works with physically challenged children. She wouldn't be able to do the amount of social work she does if she did have kids of her own, and she often says, "Why should

I have one child of my own, when I'm mother to so many of them here?" So, some people change their outlook, and have more fulfilling lives.'

Ultimately, Zainab feels, the bird will fly the nest, and the joys of parenthood are, if not ephemeral, shortlived. And the picture isn't always rosy. Sometimes, one's best moments are lived in retrospect. The process of bringing up children is often consumed by stress over whether one is doing it right. Every precocious comment, every swearword, every class assignment, every teacher's feedback, every kilogram lost can send a mother into a tizzy.

'I think the grass is always greener on the other side. Parents will always envy childless couples their constant honeymoons, and childless couples will always feel they've missed out on something in life. You need to work with what you've been given.'

One of the most difficult interviews I had to do was with a woman who had been told she could not have children. There were medical problems that both she and her husband had, and not only would it be difficult to conceive, it would be almost impossible to see the pregnancy through. So, it was best that they stopped trying.

'I don't think he's ever thought what if I'd married someone else, and I didn't think what if I'd married someone else either. We love each other first, and children are a secondary thing. We thought about it for some time, and then I adopted my sister's child. I really don't think I could have loved a biological child more. Every time she says, "Mummy!", I feel like my heart will burst with happiness. And my husband is equally close to her.

She knows the truth, and tells people very proudly that she has two sets of parents. But I'm the one who drops her at school, who attends PTA meetings. Sometimes I feel a twinge, and I wish I didn't have to be grateful to someone for letting me have their child. But I'm religious, and I believe there's a reason God hasn't given me children. Maybe the child would have been an invalid, maybe the child may have died, or maybe I would have died during childbirth. You eventually accept these things.'

What's in a name?

Women discuss the idea of changing names after marriage.

In the generation before ours, the norm was for women to take on their husbands' names. Often, women had no proof of their identity, apart from school-leaving certificates and, sometimes, college degrees. Many did not have passports before marriage and, in some cases, taking on one's husband's name in a passport made visa officials less suspicious while stamping them. Some did not even have bank accounts.

Things, however, have changed. With women mostly getting married in their mid- to late twenties, changing surnames can be a hassle, even for those who do want to take on their husbands' names. There are multiple degree certificates, passports, PAN cards, and other proof of our existence that need to be dealt with. Some women—such as writers, journalists, sportspersons, musicians and dancers—are known by their maiden names in the public domain, and it becomes a question of identity.

In the case of a love marriage, things are largely left to the couple, but one suspects the families in an arranged marriage set-up, in which they are far more closely involved, may have certain expectations in this area. But it appears that families are rarely even disappointed when women don't exchange their patronymics or family names for their spouses' names.

Sometimes, it doesn't have to do with the principle of identity alone. Vijaya Raghuraman, for instance, says she did change her name on Facebook, but it was too much of a hassle to officially change her name. There was no pressure from the family—in fact, her mother-in-law still uses her maiden name. Vijaya didn't discuss the question of changing names with Dileep, and says he was pleasantly surprised when he saw, on Facebook, that she had taken on his name. 'I guess men also feel somewhat more secure when women change names,' she laughs, 'but no one really expects you to officially change names, because it requires so much paperwork and running around.'

However, she baulks at the idea of women sometimes having to change their given names too. 'A friend of mine got married right out of college, and her in-laws changed her first name to something that was considered lucky for the family. She had to actually take it on, and that's what she's known by. I was so surprised, and I found it so regressive that a woman has to change her entire identity when she gets married. And I don't think getting to pick your new name is a plus side! There's no way I can respond to a new name, whatever it may be.'

Though some families—and communities—have a tradition of renaming their daughters-in-law, it is usually a little ritual at the wedding. Most women don't subscribe to it. A Sindhi friend of mine says she sometimes has trouble remembering what the name that her in-laws gave her was. Not even her husband's grandmother calls her by the name. It was written into a plate of rice grains at the wedding, and it began with 'R', because the letter is considered lucky for the family she was marrying into, and everyone promptly forgot about it.

Aarthi Varanasi took on her husband's family name after marriage, but says men, and families, are more relaxed about this now.

'Not all men are particular. Even my husband was asking me, just last week, why I changed my name. He said something like, "Why do you sign as 'Aarthi Varanasi'? The 'Varanasi' came much later. Your name is 'Aarthi'." So there are men like that too. Often, it's the family that puts pressure on women to change their names. In some traditions, it's very important. Some people say, "If she doesn't even take on our family name, how will she respect us?"'

When she got married, fifteen years ago, Aarthi says the norm was not to address husbands by name, at least in front of the family. When a wife needed to call him in front of in-laws, she would use 'Suno' or an equivalent. Her husband was among those who dismissed such rules.

'And nowadays, I see guys are very cool. There's a definite change, and it's become old-school to ask for all those formalities. I think thanks to education and exposure and women becoming more independent, those things have changed.'

Taniya Panda is one of those who did officially change her last name from 'Papinazath'. She didn't have an arranged marriage, but says she would have changed her name irrespective of that. For her, it was not about love, or about a sense of belonging to the other person. She feels that would be there anyway. Her reasons were more practical.

'I mainly did that keeping future kids in mind,' she says. 'I wanted all of us to have a common last name to avoid all the confusion. It makes life so much easier. Also, now we get invites to "Dr and Mrs Panda" as opposed to "Dr Panda and Mrs Papinazath"—that was just annoying!'

Her husband did want her to change her name, and since she was open to the idea, she obliged. 'I feel nowadays the girls are more like "Why should we change our names?", in a sense that they feel like they are somehow being forced to do so, and feel they're giving up a sense of power in the process.'

She feels the 'hassle' involved in changing one's name is overrated. She has a Canadian passport, and is married to an American citizen. Her marriage certificate, driver's licence and all legal documents pertaining to her status in the US do have her changed name. She admits it may be more complicated for people who have professional degrees, such as doctors, but in her case it was irrelevant.

A male friend of mine, who is now engaged, says the issue doesn't bother him at all, and he hasn't even thought about it. 'If she has a really cool standalone surname, then why not stick with it? But if it's lame, she's welcome to use mine as a nomenclatural crutch.'

Another interviewee, Viman, says most men he knows would want their wives to take on their names, 'in some form or the other'. He explains, 'Some women hyphenate their maiden names with the husband's last name. Now this is the case where the husband has a true last name. In south India, the wives often take on their husbands' first names as their last name, which I don't think many guys would like as much. I think, in the long run, it's easier to have the same last name as the kids—when they go to school and people address parents as a Mr or Mrs XX. If women keep their maiden names, there's some confusion about whether they're Mrs Maiden Name, or Miss Maiden Name, or Mrs Married Name. Some people may want to get rid of the whole 'Mrs' concept and switch to 'Ms', but I think it will still be generations before that happens. A change of name is definitely symbolic of solidarity and unity, at least for me. I spoke to my wife about it before we got married.'

Viman is an American citizen, and says the name change was quite easy for his wife, when she moved to the US. 'All you need is a marriage certificate, and all of your legal documentation changes. Sure, you may need to apply for a new passport and such, but you do that when you renew documents anyway.'

His wife, Sahana, is a doctor, and all her educational certificates are in her maiden name. But she simply needs to produce copies of their marriage certificate, and there is no hassle.

Viman also feels the issue of whether a woman is expected to wear her mangalsutra or thaali is a relevant one. He points out that people do wear wedding bands in the West, and it shouldn't be so hard to showcase cultural symbols of one's own.

He has a solution for women who feel it doesn't go with certain outfits. 'I think there are definitely ways to bridge the gap. You could modernize it, maybe wear a smaller mangalyam on a higher necklace that can go with Western clothes, and still retain the sanctitity and symbolism of our culture. I think people are too quick to give up on things, rather than see how they can be incorporated in our day, and adapted to our needs.'

There are, of course, other women who feel they should not have to wear an identification mark of marriage. 'I can see their point of view. But being all right with a wedding band and rejecting the thaali doesn't make much sense to me. Now, many guys may not care about it, but the more traditional ones definitely would.'

Minding your language

Women tell us whether it's important to have a shared language with your partner, aside from English.

Among the disadvantages of the arranged marriage system is the insularity of the hunt—the families tend to search for their own castes and sub-castes, on the grounds that this will give the bride, groom and their families a common base. However, this isn't always the case. Caste and religion don't necessarily govern cuisine any more. And depending on where someone is raised, even languages may not quite tally.

A surprisingly large number of people find comfort in a shared language, other than English alone. Though Shreya is Malayali and her husband Rajiv Tamilian, they both grew up in the north, and speak a mixture of Hindi and English at home.

Gayathri had grown up in Orissa, and her husband Sridhar in Bihar. So, though they were both ethnically Tamil, they were more comfortable speaking Hindi. She says that gave both of them a sense of being at home with each other, though she hadn't been particular that a man she married must speak Hindi.

Smriti Rao never had intentions of marrying within her Konkani community. But she would discover that she really enjoyed the comfort of breaking off into her own language with her husband.

'Sometimes, we're sitting with friends, and we suddenly slip into Konkani with each other,' she says. 'It was always important for me that my husband be articulate, that he communicate well. But the joy that I found in being able to share that in Konkani, I didn't even know I had that need! I think, now, that we're programmed by our upbringing. And deep down, you want to be able to continue that, in the things you speak about, the sort of food you eat, and even the language you speak.

Having been raised in Mumbai, Vijaya Raghuraman and Dileep Shankaran found that they had four languages in common—Palakkad Tamil (a quaint, unique mix of Tamil and Malayalam), English, Hindi and Marathi.

'Often, in one sentence, I speak three to four languages. And I feel very comfortable with him, because I feel at home in these. If I'd married a regular Iyer and I'd had to speak, say Thanjavur Tamil, or if he were to poke fun at my Palakkad dialect, I'd feel it wasn't working for me, this is not me. Now, I feel like I'm in my own home, talking to my own parents, or my brother, you know . . . it really helps even connect with my in-laws, because we're all on the same page. And it's inevitable that I use Hindi and Marathi words when I'm talking, because that's what I've grown up with. It's similar to what he does too.'

Smiling as if at a private joke, she adds, 'Dileep is a really good mimic. If he's with you for an hour, he'll come back home and imitate you. And being able to relate to all those cultures keeps me entertained, because he'll do things like imitating a Maharashtrian who's learnt to speak Tamil, and there are all these in-jokes that I wouldn't get if I didn't know the language *and* culture.'

The horror stories

Brides share their worst experiences in the process of groom-hunting.

There are some women, and I must include myself in this lot, who believe that a groom hunt can be a series of traumatic experiences. Of course, one knows sensible people who have had arranged marriages to each other, but sometimes, a good match can seem like something that only happens to other people. Most women I know have had at least one terrible encounter. The good thing about these is that they'll give you plenty of stories to tell.

The gentleman missed-caller

While I didn't meet anyone in the arranged marriage circuit face-to-face, I did consider a proposal from someone I had met through work. I was 22 years old, and had just got a well-paying job, after returning to India with a Master's degree. When the person in question told me he was in love with me—at our third work-related meeting—and wanted to marry me, I told him to speak to my family, since I was neither attracted to him nor put off by him. That state of affairs would change when I came out of the studio one day to find seven missed calls from him. When I called back, apologized for missing the calls and asked what was wrong, he replied, sounding puzzled, 'No, no, those were *meant* to be missed calls. Journalists get reimbursed for their phone calls, no? I have to pay my own phone bills, so I thought we'll communicate this way.'

Locked-in

Manisha Bhave was doing her MPhil, when a family friend tried to set up a match. 'He had passed out of some random management institute in Ghaziabad. I was only 23, and I had no plans of looking for a groom. Apparently, she didn't even tell my mom this was a 'ladki dekhna' or 'meet karna' party, so I was clueless. But I could sense something was wrong. Suddenly, this family friend pushes me and this guy into their bedroom, so we can "talk"! I was so spooked out. The guy gave me his résumé as an introduction. I found it really odd that we couldn't talk in the main hall—and this is aside from being *angry* at the way I'd been entrapped—so I decided to get out of the room. I realized only when I couldn't push the door open, and had to knock, that the latch had been drawn and we'd been locked in!'

Manisha's mother was horrified when she realized her friend had locked the girl in with a stranger. 'Mom tried to tell herself the friend was being helpful, though she didn't like the locking-in part at all. I swore I wouldn't step into that friend's house ever. It shouldn't happen to anyone!'

The shaadi mandi

When Akanksha Mehra heard the mother of a prospective groom was coming to meet the family before the couple would be allowed to meet, she decided to stay out of the way. 'I found it somewhat strange that she wanted to come and meet the family before I met the guy. Obviously, my intention was to let my parents do the talking, and to stay in my room. Suddenly, she asked to see me, and it took my parents by surprise, so they didn't think to say I was out.'

When she went downstairs, the mother of the boy looked her up and down, and asked her height. Apparently, her son was tall, and had said he would not marry anyone who was shorter than 5 feet 6 inches.

'Then, she asked if I usually tie my hair up or leave it loose. I was like, is she going to want to count my teeth next?' Akanksha says, with a shake of the head. 'It felt like one of those sabzi mandis, where the aunties break the ends of the bhindi, toss the tomatoes to test them and smell the onions.'

The Malayali Frank Zappa

Shreya Gopal's first meeting with a prospective groom was in 2007. She refused to wear a sari, and her parents settled for a salwar-kameez. 'I think they were relieved I didn't insist on sitting there in shorts and a T-shirt. But anyway, there was this *pennu kaanal* atmosphere, and that's how the madness started. My house was spring-cleaned and spruced up, and all the stuff that was considered junk was packed away and stuffed into the balcony, and everything else that was considered unsightly was stuffed under the bed. Basically, all excess fat was trimmed. The house looked spic and span, but you look under the bed or the balcony, and you would see everything that went into making a disastrous house.'

Ironically, this would become a metaphor for her interactions with the boys who were uniformly 'tall, fair, good-looking, highly qualified', and often turned out to be podgy men with soft stomachs, and oil dripping through wisps of hair.

The first *pennu kaanal* started off on a sour note. It was May Day, and Shreya had just started working. So she and her colleagues had planned a fun day out, to be topped off with a movie. She was resentful about having to cancel on them. Her brother, who had made his own plans with college friends, wasn't happy either.

'So both of us were sulking about how this had been sprung on us. The bell rang. I, of course, don't know how to be coy, so I opened the door myself and went, "Hello, how are you?" My mother is standing and wondering what was wrong with her daughter. And I'm wondering what was wrong with my family. This guy had a Frank-Zappa-style seventies' handlebar moustache, and he was dressed up really strange—shiny formal shirt with jeans, and *really shiny* formal shoes. And I could smell the coconut oil on his hair from where I was standing.

I was like ughhhhhhhh . . . so, I went to the kitchen, and said, "Thankfully, he's taller than me, at least."'

They were asked to get to know each other. 'There was literally nothing about him that I could get excited about. His idea of reading was the newspaper. And his idea of partying was, "I party, but only with boys" and I'm like . . . what?! And then he looks at me and goes, "Your eyebrows have a really nice shape. Do you go to the parlour, like every day or every week or something, what's the story?"'

The shape of her eyebrows altered at that question, and Shreya told him it was none of his business.

'Then, he said something about how he doesn't like to talk, his mother's the talker in the family, and he would rather be left alone. I'm like umm, maybe you shouldn't marry a girl like me if you just want to be left alone? So I kept asking him questions, and he gave me monosyllabic answers, and finally he comes up with, "See, when I marry a girl, she has to have one hundred per cent character." I have no idea what he meant by that.'

It turned out he had already met his idea of the perfect bride. He went on to describe her to Shreya, emphasizing her 'one hundred per cent character.'

'And I'm thinking why didn't he just marry her, what is he doing in my house? Then I realized she must have rejected him too, because he's boring, he doesn't talk, he doesn't read, he doesn't watch TV, and he doesn't know what not to say either. I mean, he suddenly saw my brother sitting and laughing with everyone else, and Sigmund Freud went, "Hey, your brother's a bit of a flirt, right?" And I'm wondering, "Where the hell did this come out of?!" I'm trying to steer the conversation to neutral territory, about whether he reads, and what he likes to do, and here he is, asking if my brother's a flirt. I gave him this one look, and just then my aunt called me in from the kitchen to serve the tea. The kitchen, of course, was the hub of all the conversation. As soon as I went in, she said, "That weirdo is *not* becoming a son-in-law of this house." I was so glad there was at least one person who was on the same page as I. Because they came through a family friend, and everyone wanted it to work out—he's *such* an intelligent boy, and *so* good-looking, and this is a match made in *heaven* and blah blah blah, and I just wanted to say to everybody, have you, like, *met* him?'

Shreya knew she would have to spend the rest of her life justifying to herself why she'd married him, and she didn't want to do that.

The Coke-and-Bull story

Shreya had no intention of entertaining any more prospective grooms at home. And so, her father arranged for them to meet at a club.

'I kid you not. He was two inches shorter than me. I was wearing flats, and he was wearing those sidey platform heels. So, when my dad said, "You guys talk, I'm going for a swim", I was like oh, no, please don't do this! Anyway, the waiter came up, and this guy ordered two Red Bulls. I'm like, excuse me, I'd rather have a Coke, thank you for asking.'

When the drinks finally arrived—by which time Heels had asked her about her hobbies—he realized the Red Bull wasn't cold enough.

'I'm sipping my drink, and suddenly, I hear this voice going, "Let's share the cock". I nearly choked. And then I saw he was pointing at my drink.'

Shreya doesn't remember much else from the encounter, except for her relief at her father's return. However, they weren't rid of Heels yet. It turned out he expected them to drop him back.

The deformity theorist

Next, Shreya was registered to a marriage bureau which asked for a full-length photograph. Since she wasn't likely to agree to dress up for a studio photograph, her father seized the opportunity at a wedding they had gone to. Half-amused and half-annoyed, she posed.

'So, we sent off this picture. And I kid you not, the father of a groom wrote in, asking whether I was hiding a deformity. Apparently, my arm was folded. That's the level of scrutiny to which some families subject brides. I had to stop my dad from calling this guy up to give him a piece of his mind.'

Photoshopped into America

Since the marriage bureaus usually sent couriers addressed to 'Father of Shreya Gopal', she and her brother got into the habit of opening the packages and scrutinizing the proposals.

Their efforts paid off when they found a photograph of a boy wearing a sherwani, with his arm around his mother.

'They were obviously at a wedding. But the background is this industrial place, with a hip-looking bus stop. We found it weird. And then I noticed this was a flash photograph of the boy and his mother. And then you have this background in broad daylight. So, basically the parents wanted to convey that he was in the US right now, and so they'd Photoshopped an American background into this. And it was . . . umm . . . well, we laughed our heads off.'

The mute witness

Devyani Khanna says one of the weirdest encounters she has had is with a man who simply wouldn't talk. 'It makes you paranoid. When you take time out of your day to meet a potential partner, you hope for a pleasant meeting—or, at the very least, an interesting one. You aren't prepared for stony silence.'

This is what happened. 'So, I went and sat. We said hi-hello. And then, he wouldn't talk. He simply wouldn't talk. When he *had* to answer, he'd mumble something, and I had to strain my ears to hear. It was literally like sitting across from a stone. I tried talking to him for two minutes, five minutes, seven minutes, ten minutes, and then I gave up and decided, *go to hell*. We each ordered our food, and then I sat silent. Finally, he asked one or two questions. In half an hour or so, our food was done, we didn't talk at all, and we left. I was so pissed, I didn't even say nice-meeting-you or whatever. That sort of scars you, because you've taken some trouble for this day, applied for a day off, some of your friends know, your family knows, it's an emotional investment, it's an investment of your time, and then you meet someone like this. It *pisses* you off.'

The other side; what men want

Saurabh Jain and Viman share their stories, tell us what women should be prepared for, and what men are really looking for.

Saurabh Jain—'Marriage for men is like puberty for women'

Saurabh Jain, a graduate of IIT Madras, is one of those who married early. And, apparently, he had a hard time defining the criteria he wanted in a wife.

'So, I didn't have any parameters, not even caste,' he says. 'When I was officially put on the block, a family elder called me up. He wanted to know what kind of girl I wanted to marry. I told him I want to marry a "nice" girl. Someone he'd want in the family. He asked, "How am I supposed to know if she's nice?" so I said, "Well, then don't do anything about it. I'm gonna marry a nice person, not a résumé."'

Sadly for Saurabh, not everyone thought this way. One

of the women he spoke to early on wanted to know why he wasn't doing an MBA. 'I told her I'm a hardcore nerd, I wasn't interested in management. She told me how her brother went to IIT, then went to IIM. Well, good for him, I told her. Long story short, it turned out she was looking for an IIT-IIM guy, and if she didn't find one, she would force me into a B-school. Wow!'

But he acknowledges that it's hard to go in without any filters, simply because of the volume of responses. 'The matrimonial process is such that you get tons of responses. And there are a zillion ads out there, whether online or in the papers. You've got to set up filters, otherwise you'll be inundated. I think this, more than anything, leads to families in the modern age having parameters such as engineer or doctor, working, non-working, and so on. How else do you cut things down to manageable size?'

In his case, age was an important filter. He was in his early twenties when the search for a bride began, which worked well for him, because Saurabh was sure he didn't want much of a gap in age between himself and his wife. 'If there is a significant age gap, then one person is going to end up being a lot less mature than the other. Which would lead to problems, obviously. Women mature faster than men—mentally, that is—so, as a guy, you should look for someone a tad bit younger than you. This was the conventional wisdom passed on to me, and I took it at face value.'

Saurabh laughs that he had the advantage of knowing what the process of spouse-hunting involves. A year before he went through the drill, his sister did. 'I realized it is a humiliating, taxing experience. So I was very categorical with my parents that I decide who to interact with. And they need to pre-filter for creeps. Because, you know, if you end up talking to even one creep, it leaves you scarred and you won't talk to anyone for a few weeks. But my dad didn't quite understand this subtle point. Sigh.'

As it turned out, the interview involving his career progress wasn't the only miserable encounter he had. His dad gave out his number to an engineering graduate who was working with a software company. She called him, and asked to meet. He was working in Bangalore at the time, and so they met there. 'She was . . . well, enthusiastic. Not a stunner, but hey, looks weren't high up on my priority list anyway. Went on and on about how she and her friends all wanted to marry IIT-ians. Okay, I was marrying a human, she was marrying a qualification. Anyway. That weekend, I was in Chennai. I often was those days. This girl decides to follow me, all by herself! Yep, I know how it is to be stalked, thanks to the matrimonial process.'

Thankfully for him, his next meeting was with the woman he would go on to marry, and have two children with. They knew there was something 'workable' in there when their first phone conversation lasted a few hours. 'Shortly after that, we decided to meet. We were both in different cities, so we met up in a third city. We spent a day together, it felt good, and that evening itself, we decided to get hitched.'

Their engagement took place exactly a month from that first, long phone conversation.

'You know someone is right for you when you can share stuff with them. When you're comfortable. I'm quite informal, and she was too, so that was great. We share common tastes and interests, such as travel. So there was, like, a plan for the foreseeable future—at least we can travel together.'

Saurabh knew what was important to him in a partner. He laughs that he used to have a page online—'a personals ad, if you will'—on his homepage, before there were such things as social networks. Top of the list was good conversation. 'That's very important from a spending-time-together perspective. And also from a living-together-sharing-the-same-room-and-loo point of view. If you're going to be saddled with the same roommate for the rest of your life, at least you should be able to get through to them about your personal preferences, no?'

Stepping back to give gyan on what men want, he says that, while everyone looks for slightly different things, the thumb rule is that people want good company, in line with their tastes and preferences. Apparently, the belief that men don't marry the kind of girls they date doesn't hold good any more. 'If you're the partying type, you'll want a party animal for sure.'

He doesn't agree with the general belief among women that the wife has to make more adjustments than the husband. Men nowadays are careful both in terms of choosing the women they want to spend their lives with, and making sure that they work on their marriage. 'Hah! Tell my wife I'm not picky and she'll have something to say to you,' he says, when asked if men are less picky than women, 'And I know enough guys who care a lot about their relationships. Who feel bad that their wife isn't putting in as much as they are. Blah blah blah. Times are changing, buddy.'

When asked about sharing chores, he suggests marriage is a good way to get out of maid trouble. But not in the sense women may take umbrage at. 'Hello, we're in 2013. Everyone does chores. Really, if you have too much maid trouble, go get married—and it no longer matters whether you're a guy or a girl, you'll get help from the other party.'

He denies that the onus is on the wife to make a marriage work, whether it's being ready to move house, or dealing with in-laws, or dealing with children. 'That's very previous generation. I know enough guys stuck in the US because their better half must complete that useless PhD from some random American university.'

Prodded on the 'pickiness' aspect of choosing a bride, Saurabh dismisses the notion that one can stay idealistic about finding the perfect partner. 'Hah! What nonsense,' he says. 'You're put in the market, and goods age pretty fast in this marketplace. Prospective brides and grooms have low shelf lives. No one has the time to match things up perfectly. If you want perfection, start at least two years before you actually want to get married. Spend a year understanding the goods available. Understanding what you want. You may want someone talkative because all your friends and cousins are the silent types. Then you have this coffee date with a talkative prospect, and you're like, "Wait a minute, that was noisy!" Pretty soon your list of parameters skittles down to three to four critical must-haves. Everything else becomes "nice to have".'

While he admits that the question of 'Are you a virgin?' is still important to many men, he adds, 'It gets asked, it gets answered either way, folks still get married. The times they are a-changin'.'

Preparing for marriage

However rosy the courting period may be, once you're married, you get a rude wake-up call when you're living in the same space. 'Living with a strange person takes adapting. You could be in love for a few years and then get married, but even that doesn't prepare you for sharing your personal space with another person. Of the other gender. Who has a different set of bodily smells, and opinions on the way your clothes smell.'

He has an interesting comparison for what men go through after marriage. 'Remember when you, as a girl, got up close and personal with menstruation. That's what most guys go through in the first month of marriage, unless they've been in a live-in relationship before. The first month is very chaotic because you're experiencing another gender's physicality and emotions. Curiosity and disgust go hand in hand. Men see that their wives menstruate. Women *begin* to appreciate that belching and farting are natural human processes, but somehow they never manage to complete this process of appreciation.'

So, what women should expect from marriage, according to Saurabh is:
❖ Gastric human effluents
❖ Scratchy underarms
❖ Pot-bellies
❖ Guys in unsightly undies

'You know, the usual realities of male human life,' he says. But apparently, there's a silver lining. 'Seriously, marriage is actually quite fun and liberating for a lot of women. Lots of folks don't have control on their lives before marriage because, well, they've never known what control is. Then they get married, and there's this guy to wine and dine you, shop for you, take you around. You've got more money to spend. And your own house to set up. You inherit a lot of friends from your spouse, who are often nicer than your own friends, because you were smart enough to marry a guy much cooler than you!'

Viman—Bridging the gap

Viman was born in Bangalore, but his family moved to the US when he was two years old, and he has been living there since. He did visit India regularly over the years, since his grandparents live here. However, he says he is very American in some ways, despite being exposed to a good deal of Indian culture, as it were.

He knew what he wanted in a partner—someone whom he was attracted to, whom he could be proud of, who was different from the other girls he'd met, who knew how to balance multiple worlds, who would constantly challenge him to strive to be a better person, and who could take on the responsibility of being 'the eldest daughter-in-law' (since he is the oldest grandchild in his family on his paternal side), someone who was like him, but at the same time was not.

It is a long wish list, which many of his friends said was unrealistic, and it was further complicated by the fact that he is an NRI, with traditional leanings. Despite his frequent trips to India, there was bound to be a disconnect, which would be manifested in accent, upbringing and worldview, among other factors. Viman admits he *was* hesitant about looking for an Indian wife, especially one who hadn't been raised in America. While many of his friends initially preferred a girl from the US, some did not.

'For me, I didn't really care too much where she was from,' he says, 'partially because I don't think it's about exposure to Indian culture per se. Because the "cultural" aspect you can get from just travel to India, but the biggest plus point I had was that I had many cousins in India my own age—about ten of us within a two-year age span—and we were all close. So I understood more of the social aspect of India, what the young kids do, and what their lives are like. Sometimes, there is a fear that girls from India are either too orthodox or not traditional at all. So, definitely there was some hesitation initially, but ultimately what really helped me was that my wife had significant exposure to the Western world. One of her closest friends in med school was from Canada, and so she knew of the little things, subtle aspects of our culture, and that helps us build on it.'

When it came to his parameters for a bride, caste was high on the priority list. He did have cousins who had not married within the caste. 'I had seen my family's reactions to their marriages, and I always knew that I wanted to marry within caste, both for my own compatibility and that of my family,' Viman says. However, he adds that it was not an issue of superiority or inferiority, but had more to do with cultural identity. 'As a Brahmin, there are certain practices you grow up with, and so I knew I wanted to marry a Brahmin. However, living in the world we do, I think it becomes very difficult if you narrow your choice to your exact same community, because your options become far more limited. So I decided any south Indian Brahmin was okay.'

He would eventually marry a Madhwa Brahmin, slightly different from his own Iyengar Brahmin identity, but he was all right with that.

Viman identifies a 'theory of four', which he says allows for a good choice in marriage:

❖ Attraction
❖ Family compatibility
❖ Personality compatibility
❖ A common vision for the future

'Beyond that, in some sense, I wanted someone whose core was similar to me, but who was also different,' he says. 'For example, I'm vegetarian, and I could only marry a vegetarian—not because vegetarianism was the way I was raised per se, but because somewhere along the line, I began to really believe in it. I also love music and culture, and I wanted someone who would appreciate that.'

Though his wife doesn't love Carnatic music like he does, she did learn classical vocal for several years as a child, and could appreciate it.

One of his other criteria was common communication grounds. His wife was raised in Ahmedabad, but her native tongue is Kannada. Viman's own native language is Tamil, but Kannada is what he terms the family's 'social/regional language', and so it worked for him.

He was looking for someone who was 'a blend of traditional

with a modern funk'. As if all this were not enough, he also wanted to marry a tall girl.

One can take heart from Viman's story—it validates the belief that one *can* actually find what one is looking for in the arranged marriage circle, however high one's standards are.

He had spoken to many girls, but nothing had worked out. Suddenly, Viman's father came across a profile online that said the girl was 5 feet 9 inches tall. Her name was Sahana. He contacted her parents, and after they spoke, they passed the information on to Viman and Sahana. Like him, she too was a doctor, and, unlike him, she had had a stint with modelling. He didn't know about the modelling at the time, but had reservations nevertheless.

'I wasn't too enthusiastic about her overall profile and picture initially, because I thought she was too liberal for me,' he says. 'She got into a fight with her parents and ended up emailing me. We had some exchanges, and she was studying for her medical boards, so we became friends and talked. After I learned about her modelling and such, I became sceptical.'

He felt Sahana was too liberal, from the way she spoke. Later, he would realize that what is seen as 'liberal' in India can't be equated with 'liberal' in the US.

'Sometimes in India, they talk as if they are super liberal, to be cool-sounding I think, but it is misleading, as we think they are as liberal as women here,' he says. Meanwhile, she thought he was too 'wannabe traditional'.

'And then I got annoyed by the extra research her family was doing, trying to have people call me and learn more about me, rather than use the direct approach.'

So, they decided a marriage wouldn't work, but kept in touch, as friends. Other proposals came in for both of them, and they would discuss those with each other. They chatted for four months or so, as friends. Then, Viman had to make a trip to India for a cousin's wedding, and he laughs that he actually met another girl before he met the friend who would become his wife.

'We met just casually for dinner,' he says. 'Since we had become friends and I was there, we thought we'd associate the name with the face. We had a great dinner conversation, and then at the end, since our parents had talked a bunch of times, we decided to meet the next day, and it kept happening. A week later, we got engaged, and a few days after, I came back.'

The one thing that didn't quite fit in with Viman's checklist was that he ended up marrying a doctor. 'I wanted someone who was not in medicine, so our lives would not be consumed by our profession. My fear was that sometimes, with doctor wives, their profession may not always allow for the flexibility there needs to be for the type of life I was looking for. Sahana, however, wanted a doctor— someone who could understand why her life could be crazy at times. So from my end it was a coincidence, from her end, it was intentional.'

Retrospectively, though, he says the fact that they're both doctors allows them to understand a huge part of each other's lives, without much explanation, and they can share the day's events with each other and appreciate what the other goes through. The trade-off is that they're not as exposed to other professions or schools of thought, but clearly, one can live with that!

Now that he knew who he was going to marry, there was the matter of whether she could adapt to life in the US—a big concern for anyone making the transition from India to America. Most of us have seen images of a country where taxis are readily available, where people seem to spend all day at cafés, and everyone can apparently afford a posh apartment in Manhattan, while being unemployed. Viman feels TV and flying visits have given people a false idea of America. In other words, globalization has made things worse by replacing ignorance with preconceived notions.

'I think people watch TV thinking that is how America really is, and India is changing rapidly to try to become like what they see on TV, and that is not the complete reality of America,' he says. 'TV doesn't show the conservative cultures such as the Baptists, or Mormons, or Hasidic Jews, or Black Christian faiths. TV only shows the common themes of Urban America, just as TV about India here [in the US] usually shows poverty or tourist sites, but doesn't show the science or the middle class of India. Indians don't always see that we wash our own dishes, clean our own bathrooms, do our own laundry, and we don't really have the help of maids or luxuries that even middle class India can afford. I think in-person exposure is huge.'

Many of Viman's cousins and their friends in India are surprised that he doesn't eat meat, that he loves Carnatic music, and that he knows more about that than about Western music, and that he can speak and write several Indian languages. He points out that there are two types of NRIs—those who are more Western, and those who are more traditional.

'There isn't a whole lot of middle ground in the folks I've

met. I fall into the more traditional types, in which case, we tend to be more traditional than our peers in India, who are using the TV and media exposure to the Western world to try to be like that,' he says.

The realities of life in America would force one out of the world of sitcoms and dramas. Families tend to live in suburbia, and suburban life isn't really about desperate housewives wearing Gucci, and falling in love with plumbers and gardeners. The realities of an American wife include having to drive to the supermarket, and run errands in addition to going to work.

'I definitely thought about these things. I didn't want to marry a girl who couldn't do the basics at least. I think, as an immigrant, you want your wife to at least be able to do the things your mother can, to put it bluntly. So, marrying a girl who was afraid to drive wasn't for me.'

Viman feels the transition is easier for girls who grow up in urban India. Sahana, for instance, had her own car and had been driving in India for many years. 'Ironically, it was she who picked me up and drove us to the place I chose during our first meeting,' he laughs.

The fact that Sahana used to be a model convinced him that she wasn't quite the 'typical Indian wife', but someone whose personality could accommodate a blend of the East and West. 'While she's not overly traditional—as I am—she acknowledges and values tradition, and that's fine by me.'

But the hurdles that a couple comprising an NRI and an Indian brought up in India must mount don't stop at the wife being able to drive.

'There are lots of challenges,' says Viman. 'One is the mindset. Here, we are taught to be more independent and choose what is best for us. Sacrifice is a hard concept to accept sometimes, but is more readily acceptable in India—which makes NRIs seem much more selfish, because we are taught to fight for what we want. That's a huge challenge. The second is the involvement of family and extended family—people raised in India are far more accepting of social rules and things to live by, whereas NRIs are much more independent, and don't readily accept doing something some way, just because an elder told them to do so. NRIs are taught to ask questions and understand why, whereas in India, asking why is considered a sign of challenging authority.'

Language can become another problem, especially if the NRI doesn't speak an Indian language. The same goes with living with in-laws—many Indian girls are not willing to live with their in-laws.

'Some of the Indian ways of doing things don't always work here,' Viman warns, 'like sitting around when you are pregnant, and having someone dote on you, or making all these homemade herbal concoctions for newborn babies, and so on.'

For women who are planning to migrate to the US, especially after marrying men raised in America, Viman says it's important to not just learn about the person, but understand why his life is the way it is.

'I would say learn more about the culture, when you are considering marriage. Ask that person questions about day-to-day life, ask questions about hypothetical scenarios, talk to friends of the person you are interested in, so you have different perspectives and are not biased.'

Of course, one of the most difficult aspects of migration, for a modern, educated, intelligent woman, is that it necessitates a long period away from family before she can get her visa. The other option is to stay away from one's husband, while waiting for her dependant visa or green card to come through. It's important to understand the various options that are available to one, before marriage, because that could also help one choose how one gets married.

It is possible to go to the US on a fiancée visa, provided the legal marriage hasn't yet happened, even if a religious ceremony has. Then, the couple can get legally married in the US. This gets processed faster, and women will not have to stay away from their husbands while they wait for green cards. If a couple gets legally married in India, the immigrant will have to wait for a green card, or arrive on a dependant visa, which would have certain restrictions on working.

'I have had many relatives go through depression and such by having to live away from their husbands,' Viman says. 'However, I find that many girls adjust well with modern technology—Skype, FaceTime etcetera have drastically changed things, and have allowed much more regular contact.'

If women cannot immediately work, Viman suggests they take evening adult community education classes, or develop hobbies that allow them to meet other people—especially women from the US. That will also help them become more independent and close the cultural gap to an extent.

In addition, it will allow interaction with people who are not necessarily from one's own community, or even race.

'It's easy to make friends just with Indians in America—that too, immigrant Indians in the same community group—but that is the biggest mistake they can make, because they create their own barriers and never leave that world to see what America really is,' he says.

When asked what men generally look for in a wife, Viman draws a distinction between what men see as important, and what women do: 'You want your wife to be physically attractive—I don't know if women will ever understand this from the man's point of view, but there has to be physical chemistry to even have something go forward. A woman can, over time, fall in love with a guy she initially didn't like. And with women, the emotional bond tends to create attraction a lot—the more emotionally connected, the more attractive a guy becomes. For men, it still is much more physical—the way she carries herself, dresses, and so on is important. So without that initial attraction, the relationship really won't move.'

The next thing is that most men don't want drastic changes in their lives. So, he says, they look for women who can fit into that life—a man often wants a woman who may be 'a missing piece in the puzzle of his life'.

'The value system of a woman is also very important, because you are entrusting your future generation with this person,' he says. 'In terms of education, this is mixed—some men care a lot about this, some do not. Some men will feel that they earn enough and such on their own, so don't necessarily care one way or the other about how much money the woman brings home; other men want earning women, partly because it's hard to survive on a single income, and also because a woman who is more independent doesn't depend on the guy for every little thing.'

There are other variables, such as how well she gets along with the family—the importance of this depends on how close the man is to his parents.

However, Viman is candid about the fact that a lot of men want wives who are willing to adjust, rather than be fiercely independent. 'Most guys still want to be the primary breadwinner and the leader of the family, and women who are too independent may not work out for them.'

Do men really give relationships as much thought as women? Apparently, sometimes, they give them more thought.

'It depends on what the relationship is for,' Viman says. 'For a girlfriend or short-term relationship, men don't think. It's about the moment, enjoying and having fun. For long-term, there is definitely a lot of thought—which is why a woman's typically afraid of the non-committing kind, the guy who has been in a relationship for years, but won't ask the girl to marry him. In that case, I think men think a lot more than women do, because once women are in the relationship, that's it—they are in it. Men have to feel like there is no other woman they would want, to be able to settle down with a woman.'

That said, he acknowledges that in general women have to make more adjustments, depending on the situation. 'I have asked many of my female friends, who are all professionals, and the general consensus is that for a relationship to succeed, the woman does sometimes have to make more adjustments than the guy. And I think, sometimes, it's inherent personalities—there is an element of ego in being male, in being the "man of the house", and a woman who threatens that ego isn't always attractive.'

Viman and his wife now have their first child, and they expect there will be challenges both for her and for them. 'I mean, one parent is an NRI, and the other is an Indian immigrant. We had different upbringings, and different views.' When asked what challenges he thinks he may face, he jokes, 'Let's save that for your next book—raising an Indian in the Western world.'

What men want

When I spoke to some of my male friends, both married and unmarried, I got something of an insight into the standards men really set for their wives. Here's what they had to say:

❖ 'She needs to have had a boyfriend, at least one . . . because I don't want some Miss Goody Two-Shoes who'd give me grief over all my exes, and want to know whether I'm having affairs when I meet them. She has to be okay with the fact that I'm friends with my exes.'

❖ 'She needs to like video games. I'm not kidding. I play video games to unwind. Ideally, she should be a player too, but if not, she has to be willing to learn. I don't want someone grumbling that I spend all my time on the computer. Because what other people do with the crossword, or a book, I do with gaming. I don't think non-gamers get that. I don't want the sort of marriage where each person is resentful, because they don't get the other.'

❖ 'I'm particular about appearance. Long hair puts me off. I don't know why, but it does. If a girl marries me, she needs to either have short hair, or be willing to crop it short. And I don't like fat women. I know this may not be true, but I feel they're lazy. I take a lot of care of my own body, and I would be put off by a woman who didn't care. People may call me shallow, but you can't deny that in a love match, you're first drawn to someone because of physical attraction. Why should an arranged marriage be any different? That said, if a woman bowls me over so completely that I can look beyond all that, I'm not going to ask her to chop off her hair, or hit the gym. And that would be love, anyway, even if I meet her in an arranged marriage set-up.'

❖ 'I'm the possessive kind, so don't know how I would feel about a woman who's had boyfriends before. It's not simply about virginity. Just the idea of exes troubles me. Maybe because I haven't been in a serious relationship myself. So, I would be paranoid that she would be comparing me with someone else. Or, that I'm a last resort. The reason I'm looking to get married is that I want to share my life with someone else. I don't want to marry someone who's doing this on the rebound.'

❖ 'I don't think the question of a modern woman who hasn't dated even arises. Forget a modern woman, chances are you wouldn't find a *gaon ki gori* who hasn't had a boyfriend. I honestly don't give a shit about any of that. I mean, I've had relationships myself, and my girlfriends were not creatures from outer space, they were women too. Some, I considered settling down with. So, why should my wife not have the same right to date that they did, and I did? But that said, I don't want to know the details. If you want to discuss your exes, talk to your girlfriends, not your husband. Whether they were heroes or losers, I don't care. And I don't want to speak about my relationships either.'

❖ 'I went bride-hunting the traditional way. The parents would speak, and then we'd go over to their house, and the bride would be in some inner room. First, there'd be some polite conversation about the traffic and weather and my education and how it's all right that I didn't go to IIT. Then, there'd be an awkward pause, and some friend or sister would be sent to bring the girl. She'd be all decked up, and wouldn't look at me, and there'd be a lot of giggling, and the said friend or sister would nudge her over. Then, someone would suggest that we speak to each other. We'd end up speaking about where we studied, and the weather, and why I didn't go to IIT. In my wife's case, she opened the door herself. And she was wearing an ordinary salwar-kameez, and no make-up—at least, not like a sixties movie star, that's the level of make-up I can spot. She said hi, and was chatty, and she made us all feel comfortable, and wasn't awkward. She and my mother started trading jokes. And when I spoke, she listened. I knew I liked her immediately.'

Acknowledgements

First up, there are certain women whom I owe thanks to, and I will choose the easy way out, and go by their order of appearance in my life:

Ma: for dealing with my temper tantrums, mistaking my pernickety obsessions for the eccentricity of genius, and shielding me from everything that was unpleasant—except encounters with men so bizarre I had to write a book on arranged marriage to get it out of my system.

Maruthi: for being my best friend, for teaching me to tell stories, making me learn to listen to other people's stories, and getting me into the habit of asking prying questions, without which I could not have written this book. I miss you every day, and I hope you're shaking your head and smiling from wherever you are.

Acknowledgements

Dr (Mrs) Y.G. Parthasarathy: for starting PSBB, the school that would nurture my potential, and for taking a keen personal interest in my growth as a writer.

Mrs Chhaya Bhagat: for telling a precocious 9-year-old me that I had a flair for writing, and should make a career of it—but wait for the right publisher—and for, even now, reminding me each day that I owe her a book with my name on the cover.

Mrs Mahalakshmi Kumar: for reading the juvenile stories and books I would force upon her in Class 6, and telling me the truth—that they were good, but writing was a craft I needed to hone.

Mrs Geeta Padmanabhan: for catching me writing a poem when I should have been taking down the answers she was dictating, pronouncing 'This is rather good' and asking me to read it out in class, in the face of my arrogant insubordination. Ma'am, you taught me grace and humility, and I owe you for this and so much more.

Mrs Vijayalakshmi Raman: for insisting I could do well at elocution and debate, forcing me out of my comfort zone in writing, and counselling me every time I would wallow in self-doubt. Ma'am, you are the reason I became confident enough in my interpersonal skills to get into journalism.

Mrs Chitra Sundarraman: for, among so many other things, accompanying me to meet a publisher on a hot summer day when I was the 14-year-old author of a terrible novella I thought to be a masterpiece, for giving me access to her library of treasured books, and for believing in me and blessing me all these years.

Mrs Rama Narayanaswamy: whom I have to keep reminding myself taught me Math, and not English or Drama, and whose ready smile, cheery greetings and sparkling wit I recall with the fondness every PSBB-ian must.

Mrs Valli Arunachalam: who, when we run into each other at events, always greets me with, 'When is your first book going to be published?' even before she responds to my, 'Hello, ma'am!' Thank you for reminding me every one of these thirteen years, ma'am. And now, we can move on to my second book!

Dr Hanifa Ghosh: for . . . well, what can I say of someone who's been a second mother to me? Of someone to whom I owe my first published story, first published article, and so much more? Of someone whose unstinting love and glowing warmth overwhelm me every time I think of her? Ma'am, all I can say is that I've been so, so lucky to have you, and your soft, encouraging voice in my life.

Meru Gokhale: first, for all those wonderful books I've enjoyed reading, and now, for this book, which I've so enjoyed writing.

Archana Shankar: for holding my hand through the entire process of writing *Hitched*, for answering my most inane questions with such patience, and for such positive feedback on each of the little doses in which this book reached her.

Taniya Panda: who made up for not having an arranged marriage I could interrogate her about, by putting me on to all her friends who had.

Caroline Newbury: for making sure the world heard about this book.

And two gentlemen:

Babu Mama: for being the adoring, adored grandfather I never had. From keeping a scrapbook that documents every little milestone of mine, to emptying your wallet into mine every time you see me, to agreeing with me that the world is wrong and I'm right, you've been the grandparent-friend everyone wants, and very few people get.

Ramananda Sengupta: for being, at different points, boss, mentor, friend, and Agony Uncle—but most of all, for telling me I needed to quit my job to 'write, write, and write'.

Most importantly, I owe thanks to all the women and men who let me into their lives for *Hitched*. Some are intimate friends, and some were complete strangers till I sought them out for the book. I often gave my friends the converse of the Miranda Warning, asking permission to quote them on confidences from the past, stored away in an audio-graphic memory. Luckily for me, most chose not to exercise their right to remain silent. It was with trepidation that I approached the 'strangers', but how kind they've been, taking time off crazy schedules to speak to someone they've never met in person! Thank you for trusting me more than I would trust anyone.

A Note on the Author

Photo credit: Lakshmi Karunakaran

Nandini Krishnan is a journalist, playwright and humourist based in Chennai, which she still calls 'Madras'. Her chief qualification for writing this book is that, for as long as she can remember, her mother has been taking her to weddings when she wasn't in the mood to cook. Nandini's chief motive for writing the book is the idea of being able to tell relatives who ask if she's thought about marriage, 'Marriage? Ha, I wrote the book on it!' Her idea of an arranged marriage derived mainly from her family's frantic—and failed—attempts to set her up with a 'suitable prospect' every time she was between boyfriends. That idea changed in the process of speaking to interviewees for this book.

A Note on the Author

After dabbling in teaching, radio, television, print and online media, she wished she could get paid to watch movies, read books, speak to writers and whine about the state of the nation. Thankfully, there is space for reviewers and columnists in the media, and her wish came true.